The Scarecrow Author Bibliographies

1. John Steinbeck (Tetsumaro Hayashi). 1973.
2. Joseph Conrad (Theodore G. Ehrsam). 1969.
3. Arthur Miller (Tetsumaro Hayashi). 1969.
4. Katherine Anne Porter (Waldrip & Bauer). 1969.
5. Philip Freneau (Philip M. Marsh). 1970.
6. Robert Greene (Tetsumaro Hayashi). 1971.
7. Benjamin Disraeli (R. W. Stewart). 1972.
8. John Berryman (Richard W. Kelly). 1972.
9. William Dean Howells (Vito J. Brenni). 1973.
10. Jean Anouilh (Kathleen W. Kelly). 1973.
11. E. M. Forster (Alfred Borrello). 1973.
12. The Marquis de Sade (E. Pierre Chanover). 1973.
13. Alain Robbe-Grillet (Dale W. Fraizer). 1973.
14. Northrop Frye (Robert D. Denham). 1974.
15. Federico García Lorca (Laurenti & Siracusa). 1974.
16. Ben Jonson (Brock & Welsh). 1974.
17. Four French Dramatists: Eugène Brieux, Francois de Curel, Emile Fabre, Paul Hervieu (Edmund F. SantaVicca). 1974.
18. Ralph Waldo Ellison (Jacqueline Covo). 1974.
19. Philip Roth (Bernard F. Rodgers, Jr.). 1974.
20. Norman Mailer (Laura Adams). 1974.
21. Sir John Betjeman (Margaret Stapleton). 1974.
22. Elie Wiesel (Molly Abramowitz). 1974.
23. Paul Laurence Dunbar (Eugene W. Metcalf, Jr.). 1975.

ELIE WIESEL:
A Bibliography

compiled by

MOLLY ABRAMOWITZ

The Scarecrow Author Bibliographies, No. 22

The Scarecrow Press, Inc.
Metuchen, N.J. 1974

Library of Congress Cataloging in Publication Data

Abramowitz, Molly, 1936-
Elie Wiesel: a bibliography.

(The Scarecrow author bibliographies, no. 22)
1. Wiesel, Eliezer--Bibliography. I. Title.
Z8972.65.A26 016.813'5'4 74-17166
ISBN 0-8108-0731-9

To Stanley

PREFACE

An attempt to produce a definitive conclusive bibliography of a living prolific author, who has most of his literary output in mainly one language, would require careful qualifications by the bibliographer in the interest of honest scholarship. So much more so is the situation magnified when the author is internationally recognized, publishes in many languages, is a noted raconteur, lecturer, journalist and scholar. The aforesaid is a bare framework for the charismatic Elie Wiesel, a true "legend of his time" in the Jewish world.

In the interest of that honest scholarship then, I must admit at the outset that chronicling the massive literary output of Mr. Wiesel, in addition to the growing material of critical comment about him, has proved to be a mammoth and sometimes elusive task. Nevertheless, this bibliography is an attempt to list, with annotations, the works by and about the author. The material that appears in English is fairly complete. I cannot say as much for the material in other languages. The French, Hebrew, and Yiddish critical comments represent selections from a much larger amount. The material in German, which is extensive, plus the comments in Romanian, Hungarian, the Scandinavian languages and others, are not included. Much of the foreign material was difficult to verify, and much of it required translation to be cited adequately. I hope to return to it at a later date. No attempt was made to list the articles written while Mr. Wiesel was a correspondent for the The Daily Forward, an American Yiddish newspaper, nor for the time he was a correspondent for Yidiot Achronot, an Israeli newspaper. I also have not included any published radio, television or movie scripts.

I found it difficult to divide the work into fiction and non-fiction, because Mr. Wiesel's writing is so very autobiographical. His use of personal memoirs, introspective reportage and legends, appears in what has been called his "novels." I have often had to use value judgments in deciding whether to place a story or excerpt from a novel under the fiction or essay heading.

The divisions are as follows: the A section lists the works by Wiesel. The English translation of his books appear chronologically along with the other language versions or translations. Because Mr. Wiesel is a noted raconteur and lecturer, I have listed under "Addresses and Symposiums," whatever published material I found of his talks.

The B section lists alphabetically the works about Wiesel. The foreign criticism is listed in a separate category with a notation if the critique is about a particular work. Only the English material in section B has been annotated completely, the foreign material is partially annotated to indicate extensive or particular treatment by the reviewer.

A large amount of material that appears in the bibliography is in good measure due to the kindness and generosity of Mr. and Mrs. Wiesel who opened their home to me and allowed me to use their private collection of clippings, articles and papers. The many visits that I made to their apartment, thereby interrupting their work schedule as author and translator, respectively, I hope will be partly assuaged by this cataloged collection of Wieselania, which should be of value to students, scholars, "hasids" of Wiesel and contemporary literature in general.

All of the material in sections A and B has been verified. The clippings that I found at the Wiesel home that I was not able to verify concerning page number or volume, are indicated by an asterisk. Much of the material that I felt would be too difficult to verify in the original publication has been excluded. This refers mainly to foreign material already mentioned, that was part of the Wiesel personal collection.

Although it is to both Mr. and Mrs. Wiesel that I owe my greatest acknowledgment in the preparation of this bibliography, there are many others whose help has been invaluable as well. Professor Jackson R. Bryer, my thesis advisor at the University of Maryland, has counseled me in all areas of the preparation of the manuscript, the countless librarians throughout the country who verified and answered queries on hundreds of entries, the publicity department of

Random House who allowed me to use their clippings file, the offices of *Hadassah Magazine*, both in New York and Jerusalem, for allowing me to examine their files.

The research for this project was conducted at the University of Maryland, the B'nai B'rith National Headquarters Library, the Library of Congress, the aforesaid Random House and Hadassah Offices, and the Hebrew University National Library in Jerusalem. For my work in Israel, which was conducted during the summer of 1973, I would like to thank the then acting director of the National Library of Israel, Professor Roy M. Mersky, of the University of Texas Law school, and the research staff of the library. At B'nai B'rith I would like to thank Mrs. Lily Edelman, director of adult education and Wiesel scholar, and Mr. Mortimer Feigenbaum for the original and continuing inspiration for attempting this project. I could not have done this work without the constant support, patience and interest of my husband, Stanley, and my three children. To them I owe much gratitude.

TABLE OF CONTENTS

ABBREVIATION KEY

In the B section, containing the works about Elie Wiesel, the following abbreviations of the titles of the books by Mr. Wiesel are used in the annotations:

T. B. T. W.	The Town Beyond the Wall
G. O. T. F.	Gates of the Forest
J. O. S.	The Jews of Silence
L. O. O. T.	Legends of Our Time
B. in J.	A Beggar in Jerusalem
O. G. A.	One Generation After
S. on F.	Souls on Fire

Note: The first three books: Night, Dawn, The Accident are not abbreviated, nor are the last two: The Oath, and Ani Maamin.

*An asterisk denotes an item found as periodical clippings in the Wiesel home for which page number or volume number could not be found.

INTRODUCTION

When asked why he writes, Elie Wiesel answers with a story. "In days of old, a young Jew decided to go forth to see the world. His mother, a poor woman in ancient Palestine, had no parting gift except a pillow. 'Take it my son,' she said. 'If you come to a strange city and find no bed at night, you can always go out to the fields and sleep on this pillow.' So it came to pass: the young man arrived in Rome, and when evening fell, he went outside the city and cushioned his head on his mother's pillow. That very night the Temple in Jerusalem was burned and destroyed. And the pillow under the boy's head burst into flames."

"I only write when the pillow burns," explains Wiesel [Jewish Heritage, VII (Spring 1966), 27].

A self-proclaimed teller of tales, Wiesel has been called "the spiritual archivist of the holocaust" and "the messenger of the Jewish dead to the living." An Odysseus or Aeneas who has gone down into the realm of the dead and returned, or like Melville's Ishmael, who has earned the right to say with Job; "And I only am escaped alone to tell thee," Wiesel, a survivor of the death camps of Auschwitz and Buchenwald, has earned that right as well. His reputation as novelist and journalist writing mainly in French, is international. His most notable works during the last decade-and-a-half include: Night, Dawn, The Accident, The Town Beyond the Wall, The Gates of the Forest, The Jews of Silence, Legends of Our Time, A Beggar in Jerusalem, One Generation After, Souls on Fire, The Oath, and Ani Maamin.

Among the many literary honors bestowed on Mr. Wiesel are France's Prix Rivarol and Prix Medicis, the Jewish Heritage Award, the National Jewish Book Council Award, and the Rememberance Award of the World Federation of the Bergen-Belsen Association. He has received honorary doctorates from the Jewish Theological Seminary of America and the Hebrew Union College--Jewish Institute of Religion. A native of Transylvania in Hungary, Mr. Wiesel is today a United States citizen.

Because Wiesel's subject matter deals mainly with the Holocaust and Hasidism, one would think that critical comment would be limited extensively to Jewish sources, where in truth, he has been hailed as a prophet of the times for the last decade.

His reputation is far wider as this bibliography will indicate. Wiesel has received critical comment in such varied periodicals as: *Commonweal*, *Encounter*, *The Atlantic*, *The Humanist*, *Southern Review*, *Saturday Review of Literature*, *Times Literary Supplement*, *The New Statesman*, *Commentary*, and many others. His last two books have been the subjects of front-page essays in the *New York Times Book Review*.

He has been called a "Modern Job," compared to Camus, Kafka, and Sartre and in a review of his recently published *Souls on Fire*, Charles Silberman writing in the *New York Times Book Review*, calls him "one of the great writers of this generation."

Eliezer Wiesel, the son of Shlomo and Sarah (Feig) Wiesel, was born on September 30, 1928 in the town of Sighet in the Transylvanian highlands, near the Ukrainian border, in what was then Romania. (The area became part of Hungary in 1940 but reverted to Romania in 1945.) His father, a middle-class shopkeeper, instilled values of Western humanism in his son. It was at his mother's insistence that the young boy received a solid Torah education, replete with study of the Talmud, the mystical doctrines of the cabala and the teachings of the Hasidic masters.

At the beginning of World War II, the Wiesel family was relatively untouched by the ravages of the war, but in the spring of 1944 the Jews of Transylvania were suddenly rounded up on orders of the Germans. Wiesel, his parents, and his three sisters were placed on a cattle train and sent to Auschwitz concentration camp in Poland. His father was killed by the Nazis before his eyes, and his mother and younger sister also died at Auschwitz. He was separated from his two surviving sisters until after the war. In 1945 he was sent to Buchenwald concentration camp in Germany as a slave laborer.

After the American liberation, which came near the end of the war, Wiesel wanted to go to Palestine but was prevented by British immigration restrictions. He then boarded a train with 400 other orphans who did not want to return to Eastern Europe. Wiesel was headed for Belgium, but the train was diverted to France on orders of Charles de Gaulle. When, at the border the passengers were asked whether they wished to become French citizens, Wiesel, unable to understand French, failed to respond and became stateless. Settling in Normandy, he soon mastered French, which remains his favorite literary language. Later he moved to Paris, where from 1948 to 1951, he studied philosophy at the Sorbonne, earning his living as a choir director and as a teacher of the Bible. He also spent some time in India, where he studied comparative asceticism and acquired a knowledge of English.

In 1948, a life-long ambition was finally realized; Wiesel went to Palestine to report on the Israeli independence struggle for a French newspaper. Later he became chief foreign correspondent for the Tel Aviv daily, Yediot Achronot. In 1956, while reporting on the United Nations for the newspaper, he was struck by a taxicab in Times Square. During his recovery in a New York City hospital, he was persuaded by an American official to apply for United States citizenship (which he finally obtained in 1963). In 1957 he joined the New York Yiddish language newspaper, the Jewish Daily Forward, as a writer of feature articles.

Wiesel's career would most assuredly have taken a different form, had the horrors of the concentration camps not happened. Because of his experiences, and the virtual destruction of European Jewry, Wiesel became determined "to bear witness, to testify." Shaped by his Talmudic and Hasidic background, he modeled his concise and aphoristic style on the Old Testament. But he also came under the influence of Albert Camus and Andre Malraux, and it was the French Roman Catholic writer François Mauriac who opened the way to Wiesel's literary career. When in 1954, Wiesel was assigned to interview Mauriac for Yediot Achronot, the two men became close friends, in spite of their widely divergent religious and philosophical beliefs. Urged by Mauriac, Wiesel wrote an account of his death camp experiences, which was published in Yiddish in Buenos Aires under the title Un di Velt Hot Geshvign (And the World Has Remained Silent) in 1956. Two years later it appeared in French as La Nuit, with a preface by Mauriac, who had personally arranged for its publication by Editions de Minuit. Translated into English by Stella Rodway, it was published in the United States by Hill and Wang in 1960 under the title of Night.

Cast in the form of an autobiographical novel, Night details the horrors of Auschwitz and Buchenwald, as witnessed by Eliezer, a fifteen-year old boy obsessed with guilt for having survived while millions died, and tormented by a God who could have allowed such things to happen. Wiesel includes in this account the watching of his own father's death. The hopelessness that begins the author's struggle for meaning in so horrible a world is evident here:

> Never shall I forget that night, the first night in camp, which has turned my life into one long night, seven times cursed and seven times sealed. Never shall I forget that smoke. Never shall I forget the little faces of the children, whose bodies I saw turned into wreathes of smoke beneath a silent blue sky.
>
> Never shall I forget those flames which consumed my Faith forever. Never shall I forget that nocturnal silence which deprived me, for all eternity, of the desire to live. Never shall I forget those moments which murdered My God and my soul and turned my dreams to dust. Never shall I forget these things, even if I am condemned to live as long as God Himself. Never [pp. 43-44].

The critical comments on Night have been overwhelmingly positive. They have been filled with plaudits for Mauriac's introduction; comparisons to The Diary of Anne Frank are made repeatedly, along with much mention of Wiesel's Job-like accusations and Kafka-like madness. Alfred Kazin (B151)* states: "I don't think that I shall soon forget the picture of this young boy standing on a mound of corpses, accusing God of deserting his creation."

Catholic comment is extensive, with emphasis placed on Mauriac's moving introduction. Wesley H. Hager (B141) feels that "this book should be given a place beside The Diary of Anne Frank as a personal record of a child's experience of the Jews during the persecution of the Nazis." He singles

---

*A or B numbers in parentheses refer to numbered entries in the two bibliographic sections.

out a particularly unforgettable moment: the Polish Juliek playing Beethoven among the corpses. James Fin (B134) also comments favorably on Mauriac's introduction. He reviews much of the historic events of the period, and he speaks eloquently about the dark depths to which the human spirit plummeted, and of the spiritual suffering and sacrifice that cannot be measured. The New Yorker review (B163) speaks of the concentration camps as one of the distinctive institutions of the Twentieth Century and goes on to say that Mr. Wiesel's book has captured its essence. M. Mauriac's preface is said to succintly state the appalling metaphysical question it poses to the Christian.

In his second novel, L'Aube (Paris: Editions du Seuil, 1960), published in Anne Borchardt's translation as Dawn (New York: Hill and Wang, 1961), Wiesel assigns his protagonist, Elisha, the role of a victim turned executioner. A recent death-camp survivor, Elisha joins a Jewish terrorist group in Palestine and is given the task of killing a British officer in reprisal for the execution of a member of his own organization. But Elisha's godlike power over life and death gives him no satisfaction as he agonizingly tries to justify the grim act that he is duty-bound to carry out.

The stark spectral quality of this honed novel is noted repeatedly by the critics. In a review in the Times Literary Supplement, entitled "Brief Encounter" (B157), the reviewer feels the book has a profound quality. "Not a word is wasted; not another word is needed; the whole is the kind of complete achievement which illuminates and in some degree enlarges experience." The protagonist, Elisha, and the British army captain are thought of as each playing a role which has been imposed upon him. "The two roles are extremities of the estates of man, the tragic thing is the imposition." Robert C. Healey (B195) mentions that the thrust of Wiesel's writing is towards the new morality characterized by the State of Israel: "Within the simple framework of Elisha's soul-searching, which has many cabalistic overtones, Elie Wiesel has provided a moving and suggestive statement of the moral basis for the new Israel."

The majority of criticism of Dawn has been positive, although some critics such as Hal Lehrman in Saturday Review (B199) feels that the past impinges too heavily on the characters in the story. Nevertheless he feels that parts of the book such as the scene in the cellar between Elisha and the officer "shine gemlike with delicate writing despite interruptions from the omnipresent ghosts." David Yount in The Critic (B213) did not find such redeeming qualities in the book. He felt that Elisha lacked dimension as a believable character: "Elisha is no tragic hero, he lacks the human dimensions for tragedy. If anything, he is a melodramatic victim, a child caught in the web of circumstance. Elie Wiesel has attempted to make Elisha the Jewish Everyman, forgetting that Everyman is No Man.... Elisha never comes to life sufficiently." Brendon Connolly in America (B190) feels that the book can be read from the wrong perspective, which is apparently the way the previous review by Mr. Yount was read. Mr. Connolly suggests that the book be read "as the objective and very skillful plumbing of a decent soul faced with a problem too big for it--and acutely conscious of the fact." If read with this in mind, the book "will yield poignant artistic experience."

The strongly autobiographical Le Jour (Paris: Editions du Seuil, 1961), published in Anne Borchardt's English translation as The Accident (New York: Hill and Wang, 1962), concerns Eliezer, a reporter for an Israeli newspaper and a survivor of Auschwitz, who is almost killed by an automobile on Times Square. As he hovers between life and death he reviews his past and realizes that, unable to confront his guilt for having survived in the midst of the holocaust, he can only escape through death now. Flashbacks sketch his affair with Kathleen against the background of Eliezer's tragic fate at the hands of the Nazis. Herbert Mitgang feels that "what is passionate in another time and place becomes falsely melodramatic in familiar surroundings." However, the mixture of existentialist ethic and the Hasidic hymn--"Babel and Singer juxtaposed against Camus and Sartre"--according to the Kirkus service, seem powerful enough.

These first three books or novellas appeared later as a trilogy further emphasizing their often combined treatment by the critics (see A4, B613-B625).

The dialogue of arguing with the Divinity for the injustices and horrors that were permitted during the holocaust is continued in La Ville de la Chance (Paris: Editions du Seuil, 1964) which appeared in English as The Town Beyond the Wall (New York: Atheneum, 1964; Holt, 1967). Lothar Kahn writing in the Chicago Jewish Forum says that Wiesel takes that dialogue further in this novel. Here, "it is man's assumption of responsibility for his own actions and his own involvement in the affairs of others which offer the sole hope for his meaningful existance" (B250).

Wiesel traces the path of apathy as it turns to evil in this powerful novel. In it a concentration camp survivor named Michael returns to his hometown in Hungary after the war to confront and humiliate a man who had looked on with silent indifference while the Jews of the town were being rounded up and deported, and whose face had haunted him throughout the years. In the course of the novel, Michael's quarry becomes a universal symbol of the giant indifference of the world to miscarriages of justice.

Critics have called this a masterpiece of holocaust literature (B250, B252, B256). Daniel Stern in the New York Times Book Review, says that the hero, Michael, weaves the themes of his own alienation into an affirmation of community. "He makes his existential leap ... precisely as far as the next human being." He feels that Michael has enacted a legend in which the roles of God and man are reversed. He calls Wiesel's writing a deeply personal, poetic style which has conjured up a painful but healing vision. "Not since Albert Camus has there been such an eloquent spokesman for man" (B254). A well-received book, Town Beyond the Wall was reissued in 1967, after Wiesel had won the Prix Rivarol and the National Jewish Book Award. The timeliness of the reissuing is stressed in the 1967 reviews. It is often reviewed in retrospect to the Israeli six-day war of 1967 (See B378). Vern Sneider in the Detroit Free Press says concerning the reissuing: "It should be included in any listing of the best novels of the year." He speaks of all the returns made by the hero Michael. "This is a novel of the mind, the feelings, and the heart. As such it is one of the best to come along in many a moon" (B375).

An undercurrent that runs through Wiesel criticism can be noted in one of the reviews of the earlier edition. It is the notion that the subject of Auschwitz is too big to handle as a literary motif. Theodore Frankel writing in Midstream (B247) criticizes Wiesel's portrayal of myth. It is his feeling that Auschwitz "is so far outside normal experience and so far from the usual categories of thinking and feeling that it cannot be mastered and assimilated." Joseph J. Friedman writing in the Saturday Review (B248) criticizes Wiesel for writing an heroic fantasy. His objections are mainly stylistic, rather than thematic. He feels that sections of the book are rendered diffuse by parables and moralizing passages and that they lack narrative pressure.

It is interesting to note that when this undercurrent of negative criticism appears, it is Jewish critics who make them. The large Catholic response that Wiesel has received has been wholeheartedly laudatory. This observation will be expanded later in an over-view of critical comment.

The proper attitude of man in a world God has abandoned is Wiesel's focus in his fifth novel, Gates of the Forest. More complex than his earlier works, this novel appeared in French as Les Portes de la Fôret (Paris: Editions du Seuil, 1966), translated into English by Frances Frenaye and published by Holt in 1966. The protagonist, Gregor, the sole survivor among Jews of his village, hides in a Transylvanian mountain cave, then takes refuge in a town, where he portrays Judas Iscariat in a passion play and is nearly killed by the townspeople when he proclaims that Judas, rather than Christ, is the tragic victim of history. He later joins a partisan group and finally settles in the United States, where he comes to terms with himself and concludes that "the Messiah isn't one man ... he's all men." Harry Cargas, writing in the St. Louis Globe-Democrat, focuses on this statement in his discussion of the Chosen People concept. In his appraisal of the author he states: "Few writers need to be read totally. Wiesel is one. It is almost as if our own salvation were bound up in his" (B269).

Comparison to Camus, appears in many of the in-depth reviews. Robert Alter, writing in Book Week, states that like Camus', Wiesel's fiction is built around a series of ultimate confrontations. "His [Wiesel's] novels arraign God, question Him and His ways, struggle to redefine Him and to recast in the imagination what man's place vis-à-vis God should be" (B259).

These confrontations occur to young Gregor as he proceeds on his rite du passage. He emerges from darkness into the light, from youth to manhood, from hate to love. Eliot Fremont-Smith, in the New York Times, feels that Gregor's search is similar to the author's. It is the theme of how to be witness. In this book, the reviewer claims "all men are witnesses, all men are Jews." He continues, "it is the condition of our lives and the song and dagger of Elie Wiesel's art" (B284).

The Hasidic folk-lore that Wiesel weaves into the narrative and which he uses to portray Jews with a passion, receives poignant comment. Desmond MacNamara in the

London New Statesman says that "the thickets of Hasidic symbolism are very dense, though they bloom exotically." He qualifies his comments by saying: "it is hard at times for a goy to follow him" (B305). Renee Winegarten in the London Jewish Observer and MidEast Review says that Wiesel "has found that the only way to encompass the unspeakable experiences of his youth is not through the unadorned recital of fact favored by some, but through the cryptic poetry of Hasidic allegory, familiar to him from childhood." His use of French logical thought in addition to Hasidic logic of the spirit combine, according to this account, "to form a combination of cabbalistic mysticism with the questing dialectic of contemporary French humanism" (B344). The overwhelming praise for this book thematically and stylistically, also makes much note of Wiesel's hopeful conclusions. After the author has Gregor wrestle with his conscience, his inner soul and his troubled love, he comes up with the following conclusions, according to Henry Levy, in the Baltimore Sun: "that life is worth living, that you can't escape into solitude, that darkness is man's lot as well as light." He calls the book "a paean of faith" (B302).

The persecution of Soviet Jews, and the apparent indifference of world opinion to their fate, exercised Elie Wiesel long before World Jewry as a whole became incensed for its brethren. During the High Holy Day season of 1965, he visited the Soviet Union, speaking with several hundred Jews in five cities. His report of those encounters appeared first in Hebrew, as a series of articles in Yediot Achronot. Translated into English by Neal Kosady, it was published under the title The Jews of Silence: A Personal Report on Soviet Jewry (New York: Holt, 1966), and it appeared in part in the Saturday Evening Post (November 19, 1966). Although Wiesel saw some hopeful signs, such as the celebration of the Feast of Simchat Torah by some 30,000 young people in front of Moscow's Great Synagogue, on the whole he was depressed by the plight of the Soviet Union's 3,000,000 Jews. To him they seemed like aliens in their own country, many of them haunted by a persistent fear. "What torments me most is not the Jews of Silence I met in Russia, but the silence of the Jews I live among today," he wrote in his report.

Many reviewers of the book used the opportunity to acquaint their readership with historical background on the Jews of Russia. In dealing with the scope of ethnic persecution, Abraham Brumberg, in The Reporter, feels that Wiesel has been able to convey the most essential truth about the Soviet Union, "that irrespective of the parallels to other suspect groups, the Jews are subjected to maltreatment and repression because they are Jews and as Jews" (B339). This view is upheld by many of the critics. Although it is Wiesel's concise reportage that receives much attention, his existential world view is noted frequently as well. David Pryce-Jones, writing in the London Telegraph, says: "The Jews of Silence throbs with the pain and the hope which he [Wiesel] feels will grow out of that pain. He gropes for insight into what it means to believe in God, to be a Jew, to overcome enemies and yet remain humane. As he gropes, he ceases to be a novelist and a visitor to Russia. His report becomes something devotional, a bearing of witness, a prayer" (B357). The New Yorker review says the book is not journalistic but "subjective and poetic" (B354). The existential quality of the book can also be evidenced in the use of silence as a high frequency word in his books. Lothar Kahn, in the American Zionist, notes that silence is also the language of the dead (Auschwitz) and it is also the language of the witness. He notes, as do most reviews of this book, Wiesel's concern with the eyes of Soviet Jews (B346). The piercing quality of their gaze gives the book much of its intense quality. Isaac Bashevis Singer, in the New York Times Book Review, calls The Jews of Silence "one passionate outcry, both in content and in style." He sums up Wiesel's message from Soviet Jews to World Jewry by quoting from the book: "cry out, cry out, until you have no more strength to cry" (B363).

Anti-Semitism in the Soviet Union is also the theme of Wiesel's play Zalmen ou La Folie de Dieu (Paris: Editions du Seuil, 1968), which was produced on French national radio by "France-Culture." This play was given its world premiere in English as The Madness of God at Arena Stage, Washington, D.C., in May of 1974. The advance publicity compared it to S. L. Ansky's The Dybbuk in its dramatic intensity.

Wiesel's literary genius became known to a larger populous when in November 1968 he won one of France's most distinguished literary awards, the Prix Medicis, for his next novel, Le Mendiant de Jérusalem (Paris: Editions du Seuil, 1968) published in English as A Beggar in Jerusalem (New York: Random House, 1970), translated by Lily Edelman.

Wiesel's literary reputation in France exceeds by far in intellectual appraisal the type of glowing comment he receives in the United States. With full cognizance of that fact, this critique will nevertheless focus on the English criticism which makes up the bulk of the bibliography about Wiesel. Hopefully, others will use the French material provided here. Jean Blot's "The Jewish Novel in France" (B13), the article "Le Témoignage d'Elie Wiesel" (B80), and "Elie Wiesel: Qui Fut Cet Enfant Juif," by Jean Ziegler (B88), are a few of the articles that I have cited that deal with Mr. Wiesel's considerable French following.

A leading bestseller both in France and in the United States, A Beggar in Jerusalem centers around the Israeli Arab six-day war of June 1967, when according to Wiesel, the Jews rediscovered their collective manhood and experienced one of their "finest hours." The book, he continues, "aims to be all-encompassing, on all levels. It ... is neither novel nor anti-novel, neither fiction nor autobiography, neither poem nor prose--it is all this together. It is an adventure of one madman, who one night saw not the end of all things, but their beginning."

The novel's protagonist, David, sits in the shadow of the Wailing Wall in Jerusalem after the victory and waits for his friend, the Messiah-like Katriel, who has been lost in the war. In his own narration and those of his companions, David virtually relives the Jewish past culminating in Israel's capture of the Old City of Jerusalem. Although the book ends on a hopeful note, Wiesel concludes that "victory does not prevent suffering from having existed, nor death from having taken its toll."

The amalgam of suffering and joy so prominent in the Old Testament, so reminiscent of Keats' "Endymion," so part of the existential writers Camus and Kafka's ethic, soars in Wiesel's Beggar in Jerusalem. In this book the author succeeds in interlacing all his themes in a panorama of Jewish experience displayed by mad beggars before the Western Wall in Jerusalem. As Faulkner uses his Yoknapatawpha County to portray the microcosm of human situations in his family setting to understand the larger macrocosm of humanity, so does Wiesel use his shtetl (village) of Sighet, high in the Carpathians, as his microcosm to view the world. Only Wiesel's world was shattered by an unbelievable tragedy, the holocaust, in which six million Jews lost their lives. Faulkner in projecting his town, mythical county, and the rise of Snopesism, need not speak of loss and constant searching in a tragic sense as Wiesel must to gain an understanding of what occurred. Wiesel finds his village again as he describes it in one of the most moving passages of the book:

> Jerusalem: the face visible yet hidden, the sap and the blood of all that makes us live or renounce life. The spark flashing in the darkness, the murmur rustling through shouts of happiness and joy. A new name, a secret. For the exiled a prayer. For all others a promise. Jerusalem: seventeen times destroyed yet never erased. The symbol of survival. Jerusalem: the city which miraculously transforms man into pilgrim: no one can enter it and go away unchanged.
>
> For me, it is also a little town somewhere in Transylvania, lost in the Carpathians, where, captivated as much by mystery as by truth, a Jewish child studies the Talmud and is dazzled by the richness, the melancholy of its universe made up of legend [pp. 11-12].

To appreciate this heart-rending full circle of experience, one would think that to be Jewish would be a necessary prerequisite for the discerning reader. Nevertheless the universality of the theme "to go to Jerusalem is to go home," has received special treatment by non-Jewish critics. John W. Dixon in a review entitled "Voice of Ecstacy" in Christian Century deals with it extensively (B442). He goes on to call Beggar in Jerusalem one of the most beautiful books he has ever read. "Only the Jews in our day speak with such a voice, the voice of ecstasy, in the will of God. The cruelty of Christendom helped form such a voice in pain." Lily Edelman, whose translation of the book has received fine comment and who holds an eminent place in Jewish letters, says in the National Jewish Monthly that: "Elie Wiesel emerges as the contemporary Jewish writer who has turned Jewish defeat into triumph and Jewish suffering into eternal life" (B443).

In the midst of overwhelming praise which includes allusions to Milton's Paradise Lost (B449), and a comparison to a chanson de geste like the Song of Roland (B459), comes a biting invective by D. J. Enright in London Magazine. He calls the tone throughout "so pretentious and portentous," the writing is referred to as "larded with meaningless mysteries and ill-timed or ill-judged aphorisms." He feels that the award of the Prix Medicis must have been motivated "by feelings of guilt or sympathy rather than literary feelings" (B445). Curt Leviant in the Saturday Review (B467) also takes exception to Wiesel's complicated stylistics. He says that "Wiesel's fusion of disparate subgenres and styles" (which include folktales, myths, epigrams, philosophic dialogue, history and journalism) resulted in "brilliant fragments" rather than "an organic whole." But David Stern in Book World (B499) called the book "a spiritual adventure so profound that it demands to be judged in terms of major world literature. Wiesel has taken the Jew as his metaphor ... and his reality ... in order to unite a moral and aesthetic vision in terms of all men." John Leonard in the New York Times (B466) comments on the quality of Wiesel's writing as well: "So charged, so subtle, so superb is Mr. Wiesel's prose style, so dangerously lucid, that his memory becomes our reality; we wake up obliged to live his bad dream, as beggars asking for an innocence we never earned."

The concise, stark imagery that is a touchstone of Wiesel's art can be seen in fine form in his two volumes of short stories, the first of which, Le Chants des Morts (Paris: Editions du Seuil, 1966)--or, Legends of Our Time (New York: Holt, 1968)--preceded Beggar in Jerusalem, and the second, Entre Deux Soleils (1970)--or, One Generation After (New York: Random House, 1970)--succeeded it.

Legends of Our Time, which is written in anecdotal form, contains autobiographical fragments such as "The Death of My Father" and "My Teachers"; introspective reportage: "The Last Return" and "The Wandering Jew"; and reflective essays like "Moscow Revisited" and "The Guilt We Share"--all of which are in some way related to the destruction of European Jewry.

These stories, as well as the others in the collection, are singled out for particular criticism by reviewers. Neal Ascherson writing in The New York Review of Books (B382) notes especially "The Wandering Jew" "Appointment with Hate," and "An Old Acquaintance." He calls the volume, "writing of the highest quality." He continues: "It is also history: the final light of art upon that unbearable controversy about those who went unresisting to their death." Michael J. Bandler in The Christian Science Monitor (B383) continues in a similar vein. He calls Wiesel "the literary laureate of the holocaust, the sweetest singer of the most bitter and tragic era of our times." Hugh Nissenson in the New York Times Book Review (B406) says that in Legends of Our Time Wiesel's writing has attained the quality of deeds. "They are equivalent to Mitzvot, those injunctions of the Torah performed by religious Jews to sanctify the world."

The individual stories appeared prior to publication and were reprinted subsequently in a variety of publications in French, Hebrew and English (see A section). One story, "The Last Return," was cited by Daniel Stern in Book World (B420) with the prediction that it would become a classic. It originally appeared in Commentary, and then was reprinted in Best Magazine Articles. In this story the author returns to his village of Sighet. He states: "My journey to the source of all events had been merely a journey to nothingness. For it never existed. This town that had once been mine" (p. 164). It wasn't until the subsequent publication of Beggar in Jerusalem, which postdates the Israeli six-day war, that the circle closes and Wiesel finds that village in Jerusalem.

The second of Wiesel's two books of short stories, One Generation After, marks the twenty-fifth anniversary of his liberation from Buchenwald. Rather than a collection of short stories, this volume would be more accurately described as a sort of diary, including essays, stories, and dialogues. According to the author, it is his last book to deal specifically with Nazism; he intends, in the future, to address himself to some of the more affirmative aspects of the Jewish tradition. This statement is doubted by some of the critics. Ruth Portrait, writing in The Jewish Observer and Middle East Review, says the statement that Wiesel will go on to other than Holocaust themes difficult to imagine; "... with an author so obsessed with his theme, it is hard to believe such a statement" (B529).

If critics better understood Wiesel's existentialist philosophy, it would be clear how he can shift his focus and yet maintain his experiential world view. The quotation with which this introduction began speaks of the pillow that burned under the head of the boy sleeping in Rome when the Temple in Jerusalem was in flames. Wiesel says that he only writes when the pillow burns. The continued tragedy of Jewish experience will always be interlaced in whatever Wiesel writes, I feel, however affirmative his themes may become. The Jewish collective consciousness, which is his concern, demands it of him.

After reviewing the last twenty-five years in One Generation After, which includes Wiesel's own need to speak, the impossibility of the task, the incessant probing of questioners for details, he concludes in "Journey's End":

> ... And now, teller of tales, turn the page. Speak to us of other things. Your mad prophets, your old men drunk with nostalgic waiting, your possessed--let them return to their nocturnal enclaves. They have survived their deaths for more than a quarter of a century; that should suffice. If they refuse to go away, at least make them keep quiet. At all costs. By every means. Tell them the silence, more than language, remains the substance and the seal of what was once their universe, and that, like language, it demands to be recognized and transmitted [p. 252].

The majority of critics find this collection uplifting in spirit and dignity. Chaim Potok, writing in Book Week, comments on Wiesel's soul: "It is one that refuses to give way to ultimate despair, despite the blood and the fire, the indifference and the hopelessness" (B529). Rabbi Jack Riemer, writing in Hadassah Magazine (B531), says "What Elie Wiesel has done in this book is to tell how Jews in the concentration camps, in Israel and in Russia, have given mankind a new definition of sanity, quite different from the commonly accepted concept." This notion is the subject of an in-depth essay by Byron L. Sherwin entitled "Elie Wiesel on Madness," Central Conference of American Rabbis (CCAR) (B74). It is Mr. Sherwin's thesis that madness for Elie Wiesel is not escape or surrender:

> It is encounter with a world of hatred and protest against an apathetic society. To live in a world which has become an insane asylum, suggests Wiesel, one must go mad. In a world of hate and indifference, madness is moral madness expressed in terms of one's love, care and concern for others. To be mad in a world whose conscience is unconscious is to assume moral responsibility.

This critique indicates how readily Wiesel bears comparison with Camus and Sartre, a comparison that has been made by critics throughout reviews of all his books. Harry Cargas writing in America notes especially the overtones of Camus in One Generation After, extending his comparison to include Beckett as well (B511).

With the publication of Souls on Fire in 1972, comes the following encomium from the opening statement of the front page review in the New York Times Book Review by Charles E. Silberman: "The judgment has been offered before: Elie Wiesel is one of the great writers of this generation. With the publication of Souls on Fire, that judgment is confirmed: his work takes on a new dimension that makes comparison with Camus inevitable" (B599).

The critics agree that somehow Wiesel was able to survive the negation he made in One Generation After, that "nothing has been learned" and that "Auschwitz has not even served as warning." Like Camus, he insists on being a spokesman for man rather than against him. The search that permeates all his books, the search for sanity in the face of insanity, finds an answer in Souls on Fire. In exploring Wiesel's existentialism, Silberman discusses how the author is relentless in insisting that man must himself create the meaning he once derived from faith. Wiesel differs from most existentialists, Silberman continues, by his equally relentless repudiation of absurdity. His central theme--man owes it to himself to reject despair--is culled from an examination of ecstasy drawn out of nameless faceless pain. This is done through an exploration of the Hasidic world in which he was raised. The volume is a weaving together of Wiesel's own retelling of Hasidic tales and legends with portraits of some of the leading Hasidic masters and an account of how the movement developed. It is an outgrowth of Wiesel's celebrated lectures on Hasidism at the Sorbonne and New York's 92nd Street Y.M.H.A.

The critics make much note of the mood of the book. Lothar Kahn says that Hasidism has transformed Wiesel into an affirmationist (B505). Mayo Mohs in Time comments on Wiesel's change in theme from the Holocaust in his last nine books to "religious joy, that mystical and ecstatic strain in Judaic history known as Hasidism" (B582). Michele Murray in the National Catholic Reporter says that "Elie Wiesel has written a beautiful book that hints ... only hints ... at some of the treasures of Jewish spirituality that enrich all people" (B584).

The theme of ecstasy emanating from pain has particularly been a focus of the Catholic critics already cited. Henry Cox includes Souls on Fire in his selection for "Religious Book Week" in Commonweal (B553), and Kildare Dobbs, writing in the Toronto Star, states: "Readers brought up in the Christian tradition may envy these Jews their hope, their patience" (B556). In a more extensive review in Commonweal, Michael J. Bandler calls Souls on Fire "a towering inspiring document of faith in man's explicable, yet unwavering capacity to begin again. It is also renewed proof, though, that Elie Wiesel will never forget the past that we ultimately share" (B544). A Presbyterian philosophy professor, John K. Roth, expresses a unique debt of gratitude to Wiesel in his essay; "Tears and Elie Wiesel," in The Princeton Seminary Bulletin (B66). He speaks of tears that welled up in his eyes during his Christian worship and that often baffled him. It was through the writing of Wiesel, and the spiritual expression of tears that the author uses, that helped the critic understand his own experience. The combination of sadness and joy necessary for a complete experience is expressed thusly by Mr. Roth: "Religiously speaking [Wiesel's point is] if a man is to achieve an understanding of God's goodness and love that is free of shallowness, he can obtain it only through a veil of tears. That is why tears, worship, and religious celebration go together." He concludes his essay by stating that after reading Wiesel his faith is more passionate than before, and he thanks Wiesel for setting his soul on fire.

As noted earlier, Christian comment is universally positive. Commonweal has four separate pieces on Souls on Fire. The sole negative criticism of any note appears in Commentary, where critic Frederick Garber faults Wiesel for lack of character in his book. He feels that the reader is left with only hearsay about the charisma that Wiesel says the Hasidim possessed and "with no living sense of that blazing power of intellect" (B563). Mr. Garber continues his invective of Wiesel and his view of the witness, in the most startling negative essay-review the author has yet received (B30a).

The charisma that is spoken of negatively here, and which is spoken of glowingly by others, refers to those special spiritual powers or personal qualities that the Tzadikim or masters possessed, and which gave them great influence or authority over their followers, the Hasidim. This very charisma that Wiesel documents in his book with literary style and beauty, I have tried to document in the section entitled "Lectures, Award Presentations and Other News Articles." Here I am not talking about Hasidism, but about the Hasidim (followers) of Wiesel, and his own personal charisma. These articles are repetitious, often factually inaccurate, and frankly dull. A great deal of tedium was involved in the gathering of these sources, and they are not the usual category of entry into a bibliography. I include them as factual documentary material to assay Wiesel's huge personal popularity as a lecturer, raconteur and teacher. Edward B. Fiske in a personality profile in the New York Times says that he "remains that rarity in Jewish culture, a charismatic figure without a beard." He quotes Rabbi Eugene Borowitz as saying: "He is the closest thing we have in the Jewish community to a superstar.... He is the only person who, by his name alone, can produce a crowd of people and an aura of anticipation. People come to him already emotionally charged. He is a tremendous energizer to American Jewry" (B102). His influence in France can be measured in part by the selective citations listed from the French press. "Le Temoignage d'Elie Wiesel: Un Dossier" in Tribune Juive (B80), is an entire issue on Wiesel. The Israeli press citations attest as well to Wiesel's widespread popularity as a charismatic figure in addition to his fame as a novelist.

A personal experience can be used here to exemplify Wiesel's appeal in Israel. In the summer of 1973, Mr. Wiesel was the featured opening speaker at a week-long seminar devoted to "The Meaning of Prayer" held at Bar Ilan University. Mr. Wiesel received the top billing for the evening, over that of Ephriam Katzir, the newly appointed President of Israel, who was also on the program. The large auditorium was filled to capacity an hour before the start of the lecture, with a large standing room crowd in attendance as well. The program was strictly by invitation only. The large overflow crowd who watched on closed circuit television on the lawn was reported to have numbered 1000. An Israeli heat wave was in progress, the auditorium was poorly ventilated, yet the audience was raptly attentive to a wan slight man speaking on an esoteric topic, "The Meaning of Prayer." The applause and surging forward that occurred afterwards was probably startling only to those who had not encountered a Wiesel event before.

What does the future hold for Elie Wiesel? A new book, The Oath, which appeared in French as Le Serment de Kolvillag was published in the fall of 1973. It has already been hailed by French critics as "the most poignant and suspenseful book" Wiesel has written. It deals with a small town in the Carpathian mountains named Kolvillag which exists only in the memory of its last survivor Azriel, and in the town Book of Chronicles which is in his sole possession.

Unlike Wiesel's other fiction that deals with the holocaust or with the psychic scars of a survivor, The Oath touches only tangentially on the holocaust but tells of a pogrom that took place early in the twentieth century, when Kolvillag was still part of the Austria-Hungarian empire. It also tells of a suicidal young man who cannot fathom the holocaust as he was told it, and an old man Azriel, sole survivor of Kolvillag who has taken an oath never to speak of how the town died. Fifty years after the event, Azriel breaks his oath to save the life of the young man, and realizes that he has in effect saved himself--his wanderings are now over--he has learned the great lesson that to give is greater than to receive.

Wiesel has followed a pattern in The Oath that exists in his other books of presenting two diametrically opposed figures--representing the extreme condition of the Jew. In T.T.B.T.W. it is Pedro and Michael, in G.O.T.F. it is Gregor and Petro, in B. in J. it is David and Katriel, and in The Oath it is the young man and Azriel. The bridging of the gap, the making of a whole person by uniting the two halves, has become the dramatic intensity found in Wiesel novels. In addressing himself to this type of juxtaposition, Wiesel said in speaking of The Oath: "to be Jewish is to have hope, faith where there is none.... Azriel and the young man are both looking for meaning and encounter ... to be Jewish is to be that encounter."

Many of the reviewers have used the opportunity of the publication of The Oath to trace Mr. Wiesel's themes. "The artistic journey from Night to The Oath is the journey from autobiography to myth; from experience to metaphor ... and its author has, once again, broken silence to bear witness" (B668). The New York Times terms The Oath "vintage Wiesel" (B643). As with previous commentary, Wiesel receives high praise by the majority of reviewers. The small amount of negative comment concerns the uneven writing style, the shifting of the narrative voice and the point of view (B662). Another reviewer called the style "overwritten, pretentious, stylistically self-indulgent and didactic to the point of sanctimony" (B654).

A change of pace in literary genre occurs with Mr. Wiesel's next two publications. Ani Maamin, a cantata, and "The Madness of God," a play. The cantata, the music for which was written by Darius Milhaud and first performed at Carnegie Hall in New York on November 11 and 13, 1973, has since appeared in book form, bilingually in both French and English, in 1974 by Random House. It has been called a poem, a parable, a legend and a poetic retelling of a Talmudic tale. The tale is that of Abraham, Isaac and Jacob, who during the Holocaust, come to speak to God of His people. They describe to Him what they had seen below. Their aim was to move God--to arouse His compassion, to bring Him closer to His creation, to make Him break His silence. But God chose to remain silent. And so the three patriarchs decided to leave heaven and return to the victims below.

The reviews speak of Wiesel's first venture into verse form and the driven quality of his writing. "He doesn't blaspheme in the ordinary sense--he is in the class of those who defy God because they believe in Him, children in spirit of the man called Job" (B680). It has been called "a highly dramatic story, even without the music" (B681).

The play, "The Madness of God," opened at Arena Stage, Washington, D.C.'s repertory theater, for a run May 3 through June 9, 1974. The genesis of this play can be seen in the bibliographic section under Zalman ou La Folie de Dieu (B760). The four-hour production was aired on the French public radio program, "French-Culture" in March of 1968, receiving in-depth critical comment. Translations have appeared in Argentina and Germany. A revised version that appeared at Habima Theatre in Israel was so altered, that Wiesel flew to Israel and disavowed any connection with it. The current play, originally translated into English by Nathan Edelman, has been shortened to a workable two-hour length and adapted for the stage by Marion Wiesel.

"The Madness of God" is a contemporary parable about a village rabbi who speaks out on the treatment of Jews in Soviet Russia just after Stalin's death. Washington drama critics used the full range of superlatives to praise the play: "Soaring, beautiful"--Richard Coe, The Washington Post; "Passionate, tantalizing, haunting"--Richards, Washington Star-News; "Best of the Season"--Roy Meachum, Metromedia News; "Passionate, persuasive, a heartfelt testament"--Jay Allan Quantrill, WAVA News.

These new art forms enlarge Wiesel's public and strengthen his message--the message of the witness which is not to forget. Mr. Wiesel's current project is a re-examination of Biblical figures from Adam to Moses in search of their relevance to the modern world. The movie options to Wiesel's books have been sold to the movies, and films, in particular Beggar in Jerusalem will be appearing before long. Mr. Wiesel has made himself more accessible to students, first as a Distinguished Professor at the City College of New York in 1972 and now as a permanent member of the faculty of Jewish Studies at the City College of New York.

In compiling this voluminous amount of material on Wiesel, I was struck by the lack of notice Mr. Wiesel has received from the established bibliographic sources. The upcoming edition of P.M.L.A. has only two listings on Wiesel. I also did not find any book-length work devoted exclusively to Wiesel. It is my prediction that Wiesel's critical image will become increasingly more universal, and as he receives a wider and more varied reading audience, he will become a leading figure in contemporary literature and letters in addition to being the laureate of Jewish literature. His nomination by Harry Cargas of Commonweal for the Nobel Prize is a small testament to that fact.

When I began this bibliography and was privileged to work directly from Mr. Wiesel's apartment, I tried to convey to the author my reasons for attempting so vast a project. I told him of the value of catalogued criticism for the purposes of scholarship; unconvinced, Mr. Wiesel shook his head and said: "The work must stand on its own--the rest is echo and echoes fade quickly."

It is my contention that a man of forty-six who has already gathered so many echoes, and who is at the height of his prolificacy, will be the source of endless echoes to come.

Section A

WORKS BY ELIE WIESEL

BOOKS

A 1 Un di Velt Hot Geshvign (And the World Has Remained Silent). Buenos Aires: Y el Mundo Callaba, Central Farbond Fun Poylishe Yidn in Argentina, 1956.
Personal narratives. World War 1939-45. Appeared in abbreviated version as La Nuit (A2).

A 2 La Nuit, préface de François Mauriac. Paris: Editions de Minuit, 1958, 1960.
Originally appeared in a more expanded version in Yiddish (A1).
Night, foreword by François Mauriac, trans. Stella Rodway. New York: Hill and Wang, 1960; London: MacGibbon and Kee, 1960; New York: Pyramid Books, 1961; New York: Bard/Avon, 1969, 1972; London: Fontana, 1972.
De Nacht, trans. Nini Brunt. Amsterdam: Querido, 1961.
Ha Lailah, trans. Chaim Guri. Tel Aviv: Ktzin Chanuch Roshi, 1966.

A 3 L'Aube [récit]. Paris: Editions du Seuil, 1960.
De Dageraad, trans. Jan Hardenberg. Hilversum, The Netherlands: De Boer, 1961; Antwerp: De Brand, 1961.
Dawn, trans. Anne Borchardt. New York: Hill and Wang, 1961.
Dawn, trans. Frances Frenaye. London: MacGibbon and Kee, 1961; New York: Avon Books, 1970.
Dawn (serialized). New York Post, beginning Oct. 2, 1961, page 28.

A 4 Le Jour [roman]. Paris: Edition du Seuil, 1961.
De Dag, trans. Jan Hardenberg. Hilversum, Netherlands: De Boer, 1962.

The Accident, trans. Anne Borchardt. New York: Hill and Wang, 1962; New York: Bard/Avon, 1970. English translation of Le Jour.

Trilogies of A2, A3, and A4 have appeared as: De Nacht zu Begraben, Elischa (Trilogie: Nacht, Morgengrauen, Tag), trans. Curt-Meyer-Clason. Munich: Bechtle, 1962. (from French) Also as: Im Sahar (Hebrew). The three books in Hebrew are Ha Lailah, Ha Sachar and Ha Yom. Ha Lailah trans. from the French by Chaim Guri, Ha Sachar and Ha Yom trans. from the French by Yeshyahu Ben-Porat. Tel Aviv: Adi, 1964. Also as: La Nuit, préface de François Mauriac, L'Aube, Le Jour, Paris: Editions du Seuil, 1969. Also as: Night, Dawn, The Accident: Three Tales by Elie Wiesel. New York: Hill and Wang, 1972.

A 5 La Ville de la Chance [roman]. Paris: Editions du Seuil, 1962.

Gezeiten Des Schweigens, trans. Curt Mayer-Clason. Munich: Bechtle, 1962.

Ir Ha Mazal, trans. from French by Tsvi Arad. Tel Aviv: Am Oved, 1963.

Lykkens By, trans. Lise Houm. Oslo: Aschehoug, 1964.

Town Beyond the Wall, trans. from French by Steven Becker. New York: Atheneum, 1964; New York: Holt, Rinehart and Winston, 1967; New York: Avon Books, 1969.

A 6 Les Portes de la Forêt. Paris: Editions du Seuil, 1964.

Gates of the Forest, trans. Frances Frenaye. New York: Holt, Rinehart and Winston, 1966; New York: Avon Books, 1967; London: Heinemann, 1967.

Shaare Ha-Yaar, trans. from the French by Yakov Hason. Tel Aviv: Am Oved, 1967.

De Poorten van het Woud, trans. from the French by Jan Hardenberg. Hilversum, Netherlands: De Boer, 1965-1968.

A 7 Le Chants des Morts. Paris: Editions du Seuil, 1966.

Contents: "La Mort de Mon Père," "Mes Maîtres," "L'Invité d'un Soir," "L'Orphelin," "Yom Kipour, le Jour Sans Pardon," "Une Vieille Connaissance," "Barbara," "Le Testament d'un Juif de Saragosse," "Moshe-le-Fou," "Le Juif Errant," "Le Dernier Retour," "Notre Commune Culpabilité," "Plaidoyer pour les Morts."

Legends of Our Time, trans. Steven Donadio. New York: Holt, Rinehart and Winston, 1968.

Contents: "The Death of My Father," "My Teachers," "The Orphan," "An Evening Guest," "Yom Kippur: The Day Without Forgiveness," "An Old Acquaintance," "The Promise," "Testament of a Jew from Saragossa," "Moshe the Madman," "The Wandering Jew," "The Last Return," "Appointment with Hate," "Moscow Revisited," "The Guilt We Share," "A Plea for the Dead."

Volume includes short stories written in anecdotal form, autobiographical fragments, introspective reportage, and two reflective essays--all in some way related to the destruction of European Jewry.

Gesang der Toten, trans. from the French by Christian Sturm. Munich: Bechtle, 1968.

A 8 Les Juifs de Silence [témoignage]. Paris: Editions de Seuil, 1966; London: Vallentine Mitchell, 1968.

Jews of Silence; A Personal Report on Soviet Jewry, trans. from the Hebrew with an historical afterword by Neal Kozoddy. New York: Holt, Rinehart and Winston, 1966; New York: Signet, 1967; New York: New American Library, 1967.

Originally written as a series of articles for the Israeli newspaper, Yidiot Achronot. First English version appeared in abbreviated form in The Saturday Evening Post. (See A36)

Die Juden in der UdSSR: Antisemitism us in Sowjetreich, aus dem Französischen von Christian Sturm. Esslingen a.n. [Munich]: Bechtle, 1967. Translation into German from Les Juifs de Silence.

Yehudi Hadmama, Hebrew trans. from the French by Chaim Guri. Tel Aviv: Am Oved, 1967.

Los Judios del Silencio. Buenos Aires: Editorial Paidos, 1968.

A 9 Zalmen ou La Folie de Dieu [theâtre]. Paris: Editions du Seuil, 1968.

A play.

La Locura de Dios. Buenos Aires: Asociación Mutual Israelite Argentina, 1970.

Salmen: ein Schauspiel in zwei Akten, trans. Christian Sturm. Munich: Bechtle, 1971.

A10 Le Mendiant de Jérusalem. Paris: Editions du Seuil, 1968.

Ha Meshulach M'Yerushalyim, trans. from the French by Elana Hammerman, ed. by Chaim Guri. Tel Aviv: Adi, 1968.

El Mendigo de Jerusalem, novela (Version castellana [from the French] Roberto A. Gombert). Buenos Aires: Editorial Candelabro, 1969.

A Beggar in Jerusalem, a novel, trans. from the French by Lily Edelman and the author. New York: Random House, 1970; London: Weidenfeld and Nicolson, 1970; New York: Bard/Avon, 1971; London: Sphere, 1971.

Der Bettler von Jerusalem [roman], (aus dem Französischen von Christian Sturm). Munich: Bechtle, 1970.

A11 Vingt Ans Après Auschwitz. Paris: Center for Contemporary Jewish Documentation, 1968; includes Zalman ou la Folie de Dieu and Le Mendiant de Jérusalem.

A12 Entre Deux Soleils. Paris: Editions du Seuil, 1970.

A group of texts and dialogues on the problematic aspects of Jewishness.

One Generation After, trans. from the French by Lily Edelman and the author. New York: Random House, 1970; London: Weidenfeld and Nicolson, 1971; New York: Avon Books, 1972.

Contents: "One Generation After," "Journey's Beginning," "Dialogues I," "Readings," "Snapshots," "Dialogues II," "The Watch," "Stories," "The Violin," "First Royalties," "Dialogues III," "Waiting," "The End of a Revolutionary," "The Death of My Teacher," "Postwar/1948," "Postwar/1967," "Motta Gur," "To a Concerned Friend," "To a Young German of the New Left," "To a Young Jew of Today," "Russian Sketches," "Excerpts from a Diary," "Journey's End."

The author searches through testimony of survivors for lessons that Auschwitz might have offered the generation born since the war.

Ben Shtai Shmshot, trans. from the French by Matty Magid. Tel Aviv: Adi, 1972.

A13 Jewish Legends; film lecture by Elie Wiesel. Study Guide by Joseph Mersand. New York: Catholic Archdiocese of New York and the Anti-Defamation

League of B'nai B'rith, 1970.

A14 Célébration Hassidique: Portraits et Légendes. Paris: Edition du Seuil, 1972.
Souls on Fire: Portraits and Legends of Hasidic Masters, trans. from the French by Marion Wiesel. New York: Random House, 1971; New York: Vintage Books, 1972.
Contents: Israel Baal Shem Tov, Disciples I, The Maggid of Mezeritch, Disciples II, Levi-Yitzhak of Berditchev, Elimelech of Lizensk, Disciples III, Israel of Rizhin, Disciples IV, Nahman of Bratzlav, The School of Pshiskhe, Menahem-Mendle of Kotzk, Background notes, Synchronology.

A15 Le Serment de Kolvillag. Paris: Editions le Seuil, 1973.
The Oath, trans. from the French by Marion Wiesel. New York: Random House, 1973.

A15a Ani Maamin: A Song Lost and Found Again. New York: Random House, 1974.

BOOKS--Preface/Foreword

A16 Gross, Theodore L., ed. The Literature of American Jews. Foreword by Elie Wiesel. New York: Free Press, 1973.
Mr. Wiesel comments on the Jewish writer. He calls him a "Jew who has chosen the art of writing to extol or to condemn a certain way of living, believing, fighting, or in one word: being. He remains a Jew even if he writes against Jews. Except in this case, he will an apologetic Jew and an inauthentic writer. For it is in speaking about himself that the Jewish writer broadens the consciousness of others."

A16a Unger, Menashe (in Yiddish). Dar Vidarshtand fun Yiddin in Gettos un Logarn (The spiritual resistance of the Jews in the ghettos and concentration camps). Preface by Elie Wiesel. Tel Aviv: Hamenorah, 1970.

PERIODICALS--Stories, Legends, Memoirs

A17 "The Death of My Father." Jubilee, VIII (November 1960), 21-27.
Reprinted: Jewish Digest, VII (January 1962), 68-80, excerpted from Night.

A18 "Eichmann's Victims and the Unheard Testimony." Commentary, XXXII (December 1961), 510-516. Collected in Legends of Our Times as "The Guilt We Share."
Wiesel asks whether the trial did justice to Eichmann's victims.

A19 "Appointment with Hate," trans. from the French by Richard Howard. Commentary, XXXIV (December 1962, 470-476. Collected in Legends of Our Time.
Reprinted: (abridged) from Commentary in Jewish Digest, VIII (May 1963), 41-49.
Essay on trip seventeen years later to Germany. "Every Jew, somewhere in his being, should set apart a zone of hate--healthy virile hate--for what the German personifies and for what persists in the German. To do otherwise would be a betrayal of the dead.... I shall not return to Germany soon again."

A20 "God the Accused." Jewish Heritage, V (Spring 1963), 11-12 (excerpt). Reprinted from Night.

A21 "Morai U'Robotai" (My Teachers and My Rabbis), trans. from the French into Hebrew by Chaim Guri. Yidiot Achronot (Tel Aviv), September 27, 1963, p. 14.
Collected as "Mes Maîtres" in Le Chant des Morts, trans. by Lili Edelman; appeared as "My Teachers" in Legends of Our Times. Reprinted in English as "My Teacher," in Conservative Judaism, XVIII (Summer 1964), 63-66. As "My Teachers," in The Alliance Review (The American Friends of the Alliance Israelite Universelle, New York), XVIII (Winter 1964), 20-22; and in Jewish Affairs (Johannesburg), XIX (March 1964), 7-9. Appeared condensed as "A Few Words on a Tombstone," Jewish Digest, X (April 1965), 5-8. Appeared in French as "Mes Maîtres," L'Arche, No. 112 (June 1966), 38-39, 59.
Reflections on the author's former teachers all of whom, with the exception of one, perished in Auschwitz.

A22 "Je n'Acepte Plus le Silence de Dieu." Lumière et Vie (Paris), XIII, No. 66 (January-February 1964), 1-4. Excerpt from La Nuit (Paris: Editions de Minuit, 1958), pp. 60, 103-105, 107-111.

A23 "The Master," a modern legend trans. from French by Gloria Goldreich. Hadassah Magazine, LV (April 1964), 4-5, 19-21. Collected in Legends of Our Time as "The Wandering Jew."

A24 "A Plea for the Dead." Jewish Chronicle (London), April 10, 1964, p. 9. Collected in Legends of Our Time.

Reprinted: Hadassah Magazine, L (September 1968), 8-11, 36.

A25 "Yom Kippur in a Death Camp," trans. from the French by Lionel Simmonds. Jewish Chronicle (London), September 11, 1964, pp. 9, 43. Collected in Le Chant des Morts as "Yom Kipour, Le Jour Sans Pardon."

Appeared as "Yom Kippur, the Day Without Forgiveness." Jewish Heritage, XI (Summer 1968), 59-63. Taken from Legends of Our Time. (The Simmonds' translation uses the nominative case and passive voice more effectively than the other translation. It also introduces dialogue more smoothly.)

Reprinted: The Literature of American Jews. Ed. by Theodore L. Gross. New York: Free Press, 1973, pp. 324-329.

A26 "My Friends." The Alliance Review (The American Friends of the Alliance Israelite Universelle, New York), XIX (Winter 1965), 37-39. Appeared in French as "L'Orphelin," collected in Le Chant des Morts; in English as "The Orphan," collected in Legends of Our Time; in Spanish as: "Mis Amigos." Rivista de la Alliance (The American Friends of the Alliance Israelite Universelle, New York), No. 39 (July 1965), 15-17.

A27 "The Last Return," trans. by Alexander Schwartz, Commentary, XXXIX (March 1965), 43-49. Collected in Legends of Our Time.

Reprinted: Best Magazine Articles, ed. by Gerald Walker. New York: Crown, 1966, pp. 205-218.

Return to the author's village of Sighet. "My Journey to the source of all events had been merely a journey to nothingness. For it had never existed. This town that had once been mine."

A28 "A Quarrel with God." Baltimore Jewish Times, April 9, 1965, pp. 20-21.
Wiesel's concern is with the kind of atheism professed by a Detroit Rabbi. It is felt that the Rabbi's atheism is infantile, because he didn't lose his faith as a result of Auschwitz, but in a non-Jewish way--through philosophical reasonings and motivations.

A29 "Return to The Town Beyond the Wall," trans. from the French by Gloria Goldreich. Hadassah Magazine, XLVI (June 1966), 4-5, 29. Collected in One Generation After as "The Bar Mitzvah Watch."
Reprinted: (excerpt) Jewish Digest, XVI (October 1969), 33-37.

A30 "Remembrance at Bergen Belsen," trans. from the Hebrew by David Segal. Hadassah Magazine, XLVII (September 1965), 9, 16.
Wiesel accompanied a group of survivors who returned to Bergen Belsen on the occasion of the twentieth anniversary of the liberation of the death camps.

A31 "Brief Encounter; Portrait of Rabbi Morris Adler." Jewish Heritage, VIII (Spring 1966), 4-6.
Review of a meeting Wiesel had with Rabbi Adler before his tragic death.

A32 "Sarah." (legend) Jewish Heritage, VIII (Spring 1966), 28-32. Reprinted from The Accident.
Legend of a modern prostitute-saint.

A33 "Face in the Window." Jewish Heritage, VIII (Spring 1966), 32-33. Reprinted from The Town Beyond the Wall.
Legend of the silent witness.

A34 "Moshe the Mute." Jewish Heritage, VIII (Spring 1966), 33-36. Reprinted from Gates of the Forest.
Tale of the Messiah who got lost on earth.

A35 "An Evening Guest," trans. from the French by Joel Carmichael. Congress Bi-Weekly, XXXIII (April 4, 1966), 11-13. Collected in Legends of Our Time.

Reprinted: Dimension, I (Spring 1967), 23-26; Out of the Whirlwind, ed. by Albert H. Friedlander, New York: Union of American Hebrew Congregations, 1968, pp. 3-9. Appeared as "The Night I Saw the Prophet Elijah," Jewish Digest, XIII (April 1968), 59-63 (abridged).

A36 "Jews of Silence," trans. from the Hebrew by Neil Kozodoy. Saturday Evening Post, CCXXXIX (November 19, 1966), 38-40, 43-49, 52. Appeared (enlarged) in book form as The Jews of Silence [A 8].

A37 "Will Soviet Jewry Survive?," trans. from the Hebrew by Neal Kozodoy. Commentary, XLIII (February 1967), 47-52.

A report by Wiesel on his return to the Soviet Union in October 1966 for the holiday of Succot. His earlier trip in September 1965 culminated in The Jews of Silence. "The salvation of the young Jews in the Soviet Union will come from within themselves and not from us." Appeared in French as: "Les Nouveaux Juifs du Silence," Le Figaro Littéraire, No. 1086 (February 9, 1967), 1, 8-9.

A38 "Hazayon Hag-Ha Moleed." Yidiot Achronot (Tel Aviv), March 17, 1967, sec. 7, p. 18. Excerpt from Sharai Hayaar (The Gates of the Forest).

A39 "L'Invité d'un Soir." Information Juive, No. 173 (April 1967), 1. Reprinted from Le Chant des Morts.

A40 "Torches in Moscow." World Over, XXVIII (April 14, 1967), 3. Collected in Jews of Silence.

A41 "Le Témoin et Sa Vérité." L'Arche, No. 122 (April 1967), 25-26.

A42 "Words from a Witness." Conservative Judaism, XXI (Spring 1967), 40-48.

Reprinted (abridged): Jewish Digest, VIII (May 1968), 27-30.

Adapted from Mr. Wiesel's address to the 1966 Rabbinical Assembly Convention. The witness idea is traced from the author's Bar Mitzvah to the holocaust and to Russia.

A43 "At the Western Wall." Hadassah Magazine (July 1967), pp. 4-5. Collected in A Beggar in Jerusalem.

A44 "Elie Wiesel Interviews 'Mota Gur' Liberator of Jerusalem." Hadassah Magazine, XLIX (September 1967), 3, 46, 48. Collected in One Generation After.
Exciting interview with the liberator of the Old City of Jerusalem in the Israeli War, 1967.

A45 "Conversation with Nelly Sachs," trans. from the Yiddish by Hillel Halkin. Jewish Heritage, X (Spring 1968), 30-33.
Wiesel comments on the conversation he had with Nelly Sachs dealing with her reaction to receiving the Nobel prize for literature.

A46 "The Madmen of Sighet: A Story" (excerpt). Commentary, XLV (May 1968), 38-41. Collected in Beggar in Jerusalem.

A47 "Rabi-Levi-Itzhak de Berditchev--Le Révolté." L'Arche, Nos. 138-139 (August-September 1968), 50-53. Collected in Célébration Hassidique.

A48 "Simchat Torah in Moscow." Hadassah Magazine, L (October 1968), 3, 25. Collected in Jews of Silence.

A49 "Nitzahon: Pereck Mitoch Hasefer, Ha Kabtzan B'Yirushalym," trans. into Hebrew from the French by Ilana Hammerman. Yidiot Achronot (Tel Aviv), November 29, 1968, p. 7.
An excerpt from Beggar in Jerusalem.

A50 "A Piece of Parchment," a story (excerpt). Jewish Education, XXXIX (November 19, 1968); World Over, XXX (December 20, 1968), 6-7. Collected in Legends of Our Time.

A51 "Etre Juif C'Est Quoi?" Le Figaro Littéraire, No. 1188 (February 10-16, 1969), 11.
A feature article by Mr. Wiesel in this French publication in connection with the winning of the Prix Medicis, 1968.

A52 "Israel Was Alone." Hadassah Magazine, L (May 1969), 7, 50. Collected in Beggar in Jerusalem.
From his diary of the Israel 1967 War.

A53 "Jerusalem." Jewish Heritage, XI (Spring 1969), 34-35. (excerpt). Collected in Beggar in Jerusalem.
Reprinted: The Holy City: Jews on Jerusalem. Comp. and ed. by Avraham Holtz. New York: W. W. Norton, 1970, pp. 175-176.

A54 "The Death Train," trans. from the Yiddish by Moshe Spiegel. Anthology of Holocaust Literature, ed. by Jacob Glatstein, Israel Knox and Samuel Margoshes. Philadelphia: Jewish Publication Society, 1969, pp. 3-16.
Reprinted from And The World Was Silent.

A55 "Night." American Examiner, September 25, 1969, p. 16 (Part I); October 2, 1969 (Part II).
A two-part excerpt from Night: the section on Rosh Hashanah.

A56 "My Christian Encounter," a story (excerpt). Jewish Heritage, XII (Winter 69/70), 19-20. Collected in A Beggar in Jerusalem.
A tale told by Moshe, the drunkard. Its moral: no community could survive without its drunkards.

A57 "A Last Survivor," a story (excerpt). National Jewish Monthly, LXXXIV (January 1970), 35-39. Collected in Beggar in Jerusalem.

A58 "The Prayer of a Survivor." New Prayers for the High Holy Days, ed. by Rabbi Jack Riemer. Bridgeport, Conn.: Prayer Book Press, 1970, p. 39.

A59 "Lettre à un Jeune Juif." L'Arche, No. 158 (26 April-25 May 1970), 47-50, 61. Excerpt from Entre Deux Soleils. Collected in One Generation After.
Appeared in English as: "Letter to a Young Man of Our Time," Hadassah Magazine, LI (June 1970), 7, 29-31.
Reprinted: (Condensed) Jewish Digest, XVII (January 1972), 41-48.

A60 "Readings." Jewish Heritage, XII (Summer/Fall 1970), 44-47. Collected in One Generation After.

A61 "Holocaust: Twenty-Five Years Later." Hadassah Magazine, LII (September 1970), 8-9, 42-43. Collected in One Generation After.

Reprinted: Israel Horizons, XIX (April 1971), 9-12, 29.

A62 "The Violin" and "First Royalties," stories. Midstream, XVI (November 1970), 23-29. Collected in One Generation After.

A63 "Celebration in Moscow" and "A Night of Dancing," collected in Jews of Silence.
Reprinted: Let My People Go, ed. and comp. by Richard Cohen. New York: Eagle Books, 1970, pp. 13-23, 23-29.

A64 "To a Young Rebel." Washington Post, February 18, 1971, PIC, 10C.
Compares the rebellious quality of his youth with that of the youth today, and he finds today's youth wanting.

A65 "Golda Meir ou l'Art d'Etre Grand-Mère." L'Arche, No. 176 (26 October-25 November 1971), 46-51.
A transcript of a TV interview given by Golda Meir to Elie Wiesel. This film was shown on NBC "Itinerary" in the U.S. in March 1972.

A66 "Michtav l'Yehudi b'Russia." Panim al Panim (New York), No. 654 (December 31, 1971), 4-5.
An essay in letter form by Wiesel to the Jews of Russia stating that it is we, not you, who are the Jews of Silence.

A67 "Rabbi Menahem-Mendel de Kotzk." L'Arche, No. 178 (26 December 1971-25 January 1972), 54-61
An excerpt from Célébration Hassidique prior to publication.

A68 "Souls on Fire." Jewish Heritage, XIII (Winter 1971-1972), 6-13.
Excerpt from Souls on Fire prior to publication. This selection is dedicated to the memory of Nathan Edelman.

A69 "Israel of Rizhin." Midstream, XVIII (January 1972), 54-65.
Excerpt from Souls on Fire prior to publication.

A70 "On the Alienation of Our Youth." United Synagogue Review, XXIV (January 1972), 13-29.

A71 "She'b 'Chiahem Shel Hasidim." Yidiot Achronot (Tel Aviv), March 29, 1972, Pesach Section, pp. 8-9.
Excerpt from Célébration Hassidique trans. from the French into Hebrew by M.M.

A72 "Master of the Good Name." New York Post, May 1, 1972, Magazine Section, p. 1 (beginning of serialization of Souls on Fire).

A73 "Shno Hasofrim Harishon." Yidiot Achronot, May 18, 1972, Section Yidiot Shavuot, p. 7.
Selection from Ben Shtai Shmshot (One Generation After).

A74 "Golda at 75: An Interview with Elie Wiesel." Hadassah Magazine, LIV (January 1973), 6-7, 25-26.
Mr. Wiesel makes metaphysical existentialist comments on: Judaism, the holocaust, the existance of man, Jerusalem. Mrs. Meir's responses are in the language of pragmatic political Zionism. A most interesting dialogue in different levels of meaning.

A74a "Two Wanderers." National Jewish Monthly. LXXXVIII (November 1973), 4, 16-18.
An excerpt from The Oath. The section on Abrasha, a na-ve-na-dnik (wanderer).

PERIODICALS--Book Reviews

A75 Review of The Man Who Played God by Robert St. John. Hadassah Magazine, LXIII (November 1963), 18-19.
Much background is given to the real model for the fictional protagonist, Israel Kastner, the Zionist leader who traveled through Nazi Germany with a German passport and was responsible, in addition to acts of bravery and courage in saving Jews, for the sacrifice of a half a million Jews. Wiesel feels that the fictional account is bland compared with the real story. "The unadorned protocols of the Kastner trial are more powerful and illuminating than the novel into which they have been woven."

A76 Review of Idiots First by Bernard Malamud and Herod's Children by Aichinger. Hadassah Magazine, XLIV (November 1963), 18-19.

Idiots First is highly recommended. Malamud can properly assume the appellation of a Jewish writer according to Wiesel. Herod's Children is called one of the finest books written on the holocaust.

A77 Review of Blood from the Sky by Piotr Rawicz. Hadassah Magazine, XLV (March 1964), 13.
A positive review of this book of holocaust remembrances by a Ukrainian Jew, who was "condemned to see blood pouring from the skies, drowning those who believed in eternity and truth and in their inseparability."

A78 Review of Incident at Vichy by Arthur Miller, Hadassah Magazine, XLVI (March 1965), 11-12.
A review of the Arthur Miller play. Wiesel feels that one who did not experience Auschwitz should not write about it.

A79 "From Exile to Exile." Nation, CCII (April 25, 1966), 494-495.
Review of Other People's Houses by Lore Segal. One survivor, Elie Wiesel, comments on another, Lore Segal's survival. Comments on experiences and wandering from one country to another. He states that these events have been written with rare insight and sensitivity.

A80 "No Market for Jews." Hadassah Magazine, XLVIII (September 1966), 12-13.
Review of The Mission by Hans Habe. Wiesel tells of the public sale of one million Hungarian Jews in the Spring of 1944. President Roosevelt, informed of the offer, said no. Habe tells of Professor Bernard Naumann's efforts to save the Jews. It is the story of his failure. Wiesel comments: "It was as simple as that. European Jewry was not worth 150 million dollars."

A81 "Another Planet." Hadassah Magazine, XLVIII (January 1967), 15-16.
Review of Auschwitz by Bernard Naumann: a report on the proceedings against Robert Kare Muka and others before the court at Frankfurt. Wiesel includes his own comments on Auschwitz.

A82 "A Shtetl Grows in Brooklyn." Review of The Chosen by Chaim Potok. Hadassah Magazine, XLVIII (April

1967), 13.

Wiesel muses on how the shtetl did survive the holocaust and how Potok's book set in the Brooklyn hasidic section of a generation ago has captured the mood of the area. "The book's power derives from its purity.... one does not have to denigrate what one is or what one recalls to enter American Jewish Literature."

A82a "Mao Tse tung Is Not a Jew--Yet." Washington Post Book World, December 31, 1967, p. 7.

A review of The Jews: A Fictional Venture into the Follies of Anti-Semitism by Roger Peyrefitte. Wiesel comments ironically on the author's thesis that the whole world is Jewish. "With one stroke of the pen Roger Peyrefette knocks down the wall separating Jewish and world history, the Jewish people and the family of nations. We all belong to one big Jewish family." The anti-Semitic tone, and the author's writing style are criticized. "The Jews are not boring, at least write interestingly."

A83 "Allies Fiddled as Jews Burned." Review of While Six Million Died: A Chronicle of American Apathy, by Arthur D. Morse, and The Holocaust: The Destruction of European Jewry, by Nora Levin. Hadassah Magazine, XLIX (March 1968), 16-17.

Wiesel comments on the silent world as European Jewry was systematically destroyed. "If proof is needed it can be found in While Six Million Died and in The Holocaust: The Destruction of European Jewry. Both books are replete with documentary evidence, one more shocking than the other. Reeling through their indictments one feels like spitting in the face of humanity."

A84 "All Jews Are Survivors." Hadassah Magazine, XLIX (May 1968), 19. Review of The Chocolate Deal by Chaim Gouri.

Wiesel calls Gouri one of the best known poets in Israel. "The strength of this book is its indirect approach. Rather than depicting Auschwitz, Gouri shows those who carry it within them."

A85 "Was Kurt Gerstein a Saint in Nazi Clothing?" New York Times Book Review, April 4, 1971, pp. 1, 44-45.

Review of A Spy for God by Pierre Joffrey. Wiesel

finds it difficult to judge Kurt Gerstein, who joined the Nazi Party at the beginning of the war and later martyred himself against the Nazis. There are too many questions left unanswered, Wiesel feels.

A86 Review of So Far by Meyer Weisgal. New York Times Book Review, February 27, 1972, pp. 6-7.
Wiesel discusses what the shtetl and Kikl (Weisgal's native village) meant to this important Jewish world leader. He concludes that the history and the anecdotes are interrelated and for Meyer Weisgal Kikl "a state of mind" and Jerusalem will remain forever inseparable. [Note: Wiesel makes a similar comparison with his own village of Sighet and Jerusalem in A Beggar in Jerusalem]. There is also much mention in this comprehensive review of world leaders and historical information as they relate to Weisgal's position in Zionism and Jewish history.

A87 Review of So Far by Meyer Weisgal. Aufbau (New York), March 3, 1972, p. 15.
German review in a German language newspaper of Jewish interest published in New York.

A88 "The Telling of the War." New York Times Book Review, November 5, 1972, part 2 (Children's Books), Fall 1972, pp. 3, 22.
An essay-review of children's books on war. Wiesel notes that the holocaust has now become a "fit" subject for children, and how parents once shielded their children from the horrors. Seven books are reviewed: The Upstairs Room, by Johanna Reiss; I Was There, by Hans Peter Richter; From Ice Set Free, by Otto Kiep; I Am Rosemarie, by Marietta Moskin; Petro's War, by Alki Zei; When Hitler Stole Pink Rabbit, by Judith Kerr; Till The Break of Day, by Maia Wojciechowska.

PERIODICALS--Addresses, Symposiums

A89 "On Being a Jew." Jewish Heritage, X (Summer 1967), 51-55.
Test of address delivered at commencement exercises of the Jewish Theological Seminary of America, June 4, 1967, at which time an honorary Doctorate of Letters was conferred on Mr. Wiesel.

"The past does not begin with one's childhood."

A90 "Jewish Values in the Post-Holocaust Future--A Symposium." Judaism, XVI (Summer 1967), 266-299 [281-291, 298-299]. Participants: Emil L. Fackenheim, George Steiner, Richard H. Popkin, Elie Wiesel.

"Jews must teach the world about destruction in the hope of saving it."

A91 "Telling the Tale." Dimensions of American Judaism, II (Spring 1968), 9-12. Continued, III (Fall 1968), 35.

Excerpt of an address in which Wiesel speaks of the silence of Steven Wise.

A92 "Toward a Philosophy of Jewish Existence." Discussion proceeding of the Twenty-fifth Anniversary Convocation of the Jewish Centers of Los Angeles. Los Angeles, California (March 6, 1968), 3-43. [Published as the proceedings of the meeting.]

Panelists: Rabbi Robert Gordis, Dr. Moshe Davis, Elie Wiesel.

A93 Jewish Existence in an Open Society. Los Angeles: Anderson Ritchie and Simon, 1970, pp. 39-49.

Address by Mr. Wiesel "The Fiery Shadow-Jewish Existence Out of the Holocaust." The author comments on his education, on not becoming a philosopher, and on his need to ask questions. A companion volume to "Toward a Philosophy of Jewish Existence."

A94 From Holocaust to Rebirth. New York: The Council of Jewish Federations and Welfare Funds, 1970. (12-page pamphlet).

Proceedings of an address given on November 14, 1970 by Elie Wiesel at the 29th General Assembly of the Council of Jewish Federations and Welfare Funds in Kansas City, Missouri. It contains much of Wiesel's philosophy. His topics covered: "The Privileged Generation," "Laughter and the Jew," "An Act of Defiance--To Begin Again," "The Stubbornness of the Jew," "The Laughter of the Madman," "The Unanswered Question," "Where Were You? What Did You Do?" "The Missing Dimension," "Solidarity with Soviet Jewry," "Then Was Our Mouth Filled with Laughter."

Reprinted: (in part) by United Jewish Appeal of

Greater Washington in letter of solicitation of funds for Soviet Jewry, April 5, 1972.

A95 "Out of the Ashes." Jewish Heritage, XII (Fall 1970), 19-30 [29-30].

Proceedings of a symposium given on February 22, 1970 on "Jewish Writers in the Soviet Union: Confrontation and Contribution," sponsored by the B'nai B'rith commission on Adult Jewish Education as a tribute to the late Isaac Babel. Participants: Max Hayward, Maurice Samuels, Alfred Kazin, Elie Wiesel. Mr. Wiesel spoke on the plight of Jewish writers in the Soviet Union.

A96 "Jews Are You Worthy?" Daily Pennsylvanian, October 15, 1971, pp. 1, 8.

Address at the B'nai B'rith National Triennial convention. Wiesel asks the young people of today to be worthy of the fight for Soviet Jewry.

A97 "Beyond Survival." European Judaism, VI (Winter 1971-1972), 4-10.

An edited transcript of a conversation Elie Wiesel and Eugene Heimler had with two of the editors of the publication, Michael Goulston and Anthony Rudolf. The subject is holocaust themes and beyond.

A98 "The Jews: Next Year in Which Jerusalem?" Time, XCIX (April 10, 1972), 54-63 [54].

Time cover story on "what it means to be Jewish." Wiesel comments on what one must do to be Jewish--he must tell the tale and bear witness.

A99 "Jewish Priorities." Address, Jewish Week-American Examiner, New York, May 18, 1972, p. 4.

Proceedings of the American Jewish Congress held in Cleveland, Ohio, reported on. Mr. Wiesel, the luncheon speaker on May 11, 1972, told the Congress that there was no conflict between promoting universal causes like peace and social justice and protecting specific Jewish interests. "I believe that today no one is more universal than he who is Jewish," he said.

A100 "Hasidism and Man's Love of Man." Jewish Heritage, XIV (Fall/Winter 1972), 6-12.

Adapted from the transcript of a dialogue between Mr. Wiesel and Rabbi Abraham J. Heschel on "Hasidism: What it is Not: What It Is," delivered at the B'nai B'rith Adult Jewish Education Commission Meeting held at the Waldorf-Astoria, New York City, on February 20, 1972.

Mr. Wiesel defines Hasidism, calls it compassion, love, fervor--a call to friendship. He gives examples of some Hasidic rebbes' aphorisms.

A101 "Faces of a Slaughtered People: Captions for an Exhibit On the Holocaust." The National Jewish Monthly, LXXVIII (January 1973), 6-8.

An essay by Mr. Wiesel edited from an address given at B'nai B'rith National Headquarters in Washington, D.C., for the opening of a photographic exhibit to mark the thirtieth anniversary of the Holocaust by the Yad Vashem.

A101a "Against Despair." New York: United Jewish Appeal, December 1973 (15-page pamphlet).

An address, reprinted in total and distributed by the United Jewish Appeal, that was given by Mr. Wiesel on the occasion of the U.J.A. 1974 National Conference, December 8, 1973. Mr. Wiesel gave the first annual Louis A. Pincus Memorial Lecture. He wove his theme--the interdependancy of Jews--around the events of history and the recent October Mid-East War. The need to celebrate, the need to keep faith "has never been so needed nor so justified."

A102 "Are We Listening?" Arena Stage Program Supplement (May 3-June 9, 1974), 1, 4 (for the production of "The Madness of God").

The author/playwright describes his first visit to Russia and the reasons for writing the play. He speaks of the work as a testimony rather than as a work of the imagination. The setting is post-Stalin times, and Wiesel says "The deportees are returning from Siberia but terror and silence still dominate the Jewish communities. The tyrant is dead but his law still prevails; the nightmare has not yet lifted."

Section B

WORKS ABOUT ELIE WIESEL

BOOKS

B 1 Alter, Robert. "Elie Wiesel: Between Hangman and Victim." In his After the Tradition. New York: E. P. Dutton, 1969, pp. 151-160.
The author comments on Wiesel's novels from an Hasidic viewpoint. He finds his works easy reading, but difficult to assimilate, primarily because of the movement toward and away from faith.

B 2 Alvarez, A. "The Literature of the Holocaust." In his Beyond All This Fiddle: Essays 1955-1967. New York: Random House, 1968, pp. 24-33 [24-25].
Reprinted from Commentary XXXVII (November 1964, 65-69 [65-66]). See B11.

B 3 Fackenheim, Emil. "On the Self-Exposure of Faith to the Modern Secular World." In his Quest for Past and Future. Bloomington: Indiana University Press, 1968, pp. 278-305 [303-305].
Reprinted from Daedalus, XCVI (Winter 1967), pp. 193-219. See B25.

B 4 ________. "The Commanding Voice of Auschwitz." In his God's Presence In History: Jewish Affirmations and Philosophical Reflections. New York: New York University Press, 1970, pp. 67-98.
Fackenheim's writings on the holocaust particularly here on Auschwitz, are must reading for students of Wiesel's writing. In the section, "The Madman's Prayer," Fackenheim compares a tale of madness told respectively by Wiesel and by Nietzsche.

B 5 Friedman, Maurice. "The dialogue with the Absurd: the Later Camus and Kafka; Elie Wiesel and the

Modern Job." In his _To Deny Our Nothingness: Contemporary Images of Man._ London: Victor Gollancz Ltd., 1967, pp. 335-354.
Reprinted from _Commonweal_, LXXXV (October 14, 1966), 48-52. See B30.

B 6 Halperin, Irving. _Messengers from the Dead._ Philadelphia: Westminister Press, 1970, pp. 65-106.
The section on Wiesel deals with a compendium of motifs from the first five novels. Halperin treats _Night_ as nonfiction autobiography and the remaining four books as fiction. His concern is for the "meaningful human relationships" in the works rather than their literary aspects.

B 7 Kahn, Lothar. "Elie Wiesel: Neo-Hasidism." In his _Mirrors of the Jewish Mind: A Gallery of Portraits of European Jewish Writers of Our Time._ New York: Thomas Yoseloff, 1968, pp. 176-193.
Reprinted from _Chicago Jewish Forum_ (Summer 1965), appeared altered as: "Messenger of the Dead." See B44.

B 8 Kazin, Alfred. "The Least of These." In his _Contemporaries._ Boston: Little, Brown, 1962, pp. 296-300.
Reprinted from _The Reporter_, XXIII (October 27, 1960), 54-57. See B151.

PERIODICALS--Essay-Reviews

B 9 Alter, Robert. "The Apocalyptic Temper." _Commentary_, XLI (June 1966), 61-66 [66].
The author comments on Bellow and other Jewish writers. He feels that the American fiction in vogue today is based on a comic apocalypse, or a complete failure of faith. Wiesel, by comparison, after experiencing the terrible vision of the holocaust, refuses to look at the world in a apocalyptic light. He sees a messianic reconstruction of life after the war.

B10 _______. "The Novels of Elie Wiesel." _Hadassah Magazine_, XLVII (April 1966), 17-18.
A review-essay of the first five books. Mr. Alter places Wiesel in various literary genres. His accom-

plishment: "He has managed to realize the terrible past imaginatively with growing artistic strength in a narrative form that is consecutive, coherent and, at least on the surface, realistic in a taut prose that is a model of lucidity and precision."

B11 Alvarez, A. "The Literature of the Holocaust." Commentary, XXXVIII (November 1964), 65-69 [65-66]. Collected in B 2.

Wiesel's Night is compared and contrasted with Josef Bor's Terezin Requiem. "As a human document, Night is almost unbearably painful, and certainly beyond criticism. But like The Terezin Requiem, and dozens of other equally sincere, equally distressing books, it is a failure as a work of art." Alvarez goes on to state that Wiesel falls back on rhetoric when what he has to say becomes intolerable for him. The reviewer treats other books on the holocaust as well in this essay.

B12 Angoff, Charles. "Jewish-American Imaginative Writings in the Last Twenty-Five Years." Jewish Book Annual, XXV. New York: Jewish Book Council of America, 1967, 129-139 [139].

One of the few places where Wiesel is included in an analysis of Jewish-American writing.

B13 Blot, Jean. "The Jewish Novel in France." European Judaism, V (Winter 1970/71), 8-10.

Wiesel is discussed along with Cohen, Doubrousky, Gary and Modiano. Le Mendiant de Jérusalem is treated specifically in this essay. The author states that Wiesel tells a truly Jewish story "where the anti-semite and the Holocaust are catastrophic facts.... It is with Wiesel that an authentically Jewish novel in French literature is born."

B14 Cain, Seymour. "The Question and the Answers After Auschwitz." Judaism, XX (Summer 1971), 263-278 [276].

Quotes Wiesel as saying: "The divine promise to protect the existence of the Jewish people was broken at Auschwitz, hence the theological terror and confusion." See A90.

B15 Cargas, Harry J. "Holocaust Literature: Today's Burning Bush." America, CXXV (November 27,

1971), 458-459.
Review essay on the writers of the Holocaust. The reviewer calls it the contemporary literature of prophecy. Wiesel is included in this list along with Frankl, Schwartz-Bart, Primo Levi and Josef Bor.

B16 Cohen, Arthur A. "Silence and Laughter." Jewish Heritage, VIII (Spring 1966), 37-39.
"To be and remain the novelist of the Holocaust, Wiesel must show that the slaying still goes on, that today in our world of tenacious innocence and repetitive opulence, there is room for the new speech of silence and laughter."

B17 Cotta, Michele. "Oui à Non et Non à Oui." L'Express (Paris) June 13-19, 1966, p. 124.
A French essay-review.

B18 Dewey, Bradley R. "The Elie Wiesel Phenomenon: 1. Interpretation and Prediction." Conservative Judaism, XXV (Fall 1970), 25-33.
Excellent in-depth essay critique of Wiesel's works. Dewey speaks of Wiesel's theological burden, his recurring themes of darkness and silence, and his being spokesman to this generation.

B19 Dresner, Samuel H. "The Elie Wiesel Phenomenon: 2. Witness for Judaism." Conservative Judaism, XXV (Fall 1970), 34-41.
The author relates his feelings upon hearing Wiesel read from his "Jerusalem" section of Beggar in Jerusalem at the Rabbinical Assembly in 1968. He discusses Wiesel's "witness" theme, and the things that Wiesel rebels against. The question, "will we live lives that are compatible with our destiny" is why Elie Wiesel writes, "to remind us."
Part 1 see B18.

B20 Edelman, Lily. "Kaddish for the Six Million: The Work of Elie Wiesel." Jewish Heritage, VIII (Spring 1966), 40-47.
Review essay on the theme of Kaddish, the prayer for the dead. This theme is traced through Night, Dawn, The Accident, and The Town Beyond the Wall. Mrs. Edelman says that Wiesel brings the reader through much agonized suffering, but relief comes with his statement: "With God in his place, man is liber-

ated, Kaddish is said and life can go on."

B21 ________. "Legends of Our Time." Jewish Heritage, XI (Fall/Winter 1968), 3-4, 63.

In a review editorial, Mrs. Edelman comments: "Jewish stories from the ancient bottles can be forever fresh, forever relevant."

B22 Eisbon, Shmuel. "Eliezer Visel's Bichar Vegan Yiddishan Churban." Dorem Afrike (Johannesburg, South Africa), (September/October 1964), pp. 41-42.

A Yiddish essay-review chronicling Wiesel's writing to date.

B23 *________. "Literatur ... Kunst ... Farvilung." Der Algemeiner Journal (New York), January 12, 1973.

A review-essay in a newly formed Yiddish newspaper in New York, for which Mr. Wiesel is a feature writer.

B24 Ezrahi, Sidra. "Spokesman for the Six Million." Jerusalem Post, April 7, 1972, Magazine Section, pp. 12-14.

All aspects of Wiesel and his work are covered in this lengthy comprehensive treatment. The topics include: "Autobiographical material," "A subject for literature," "Hope of renewal," "Incomplete Return," "Protest and faith," "Adaptation of lectures."

Mr. Ezrahi's comments also include material on Wiesel's Israeli public role, which has been widely reported in the Israeli press, e.g., the misunderstanding with Foreign Minister Abba Eban and his political opinions on the so-called capture of Martin Bormann. This new interest in Wiesel has made him, according to this critic, no longer the witness or the teller of tales, but "a marketable moral authority in a world hungry for new saints."

B25 Fackenheim, Emil L. "On the Self-Exposure of Faith to the Modern Secular World." Daedalus, XCVI (Winter 1967), 193-219. Collected in B3.

A novelist can pose the questions of Jewish existence after the Holocaust better than the theologian can.

B26 Feld, Ami. "Kol Hashuv M'Aver Ha 'O Kinus." Yidiot Achronot (Tel Aviv), March 24, 1969, p. 16.

An Israeli essay in Hebrew giving much biographical information and opinions of the author.

B27 "Fervor Dominates Wiesel's Life, Works." Miami News, May 11, 1972, Life Style Section, p. 6.
An essay that touches on Souls on Fire and also comments on a recent appearance by Wiesel in Miami. "Elie Wiesel took the clinical madness that was left to him after Auschwitz and Buchenwald and turned it into a mystical creative madness."

B28 Finkelstein, Sidney. "Elie Wiesel's Spiritual Journey." Jewish Currents, XXI (May 1967), 22-28.
An article covering the first four books. He speaks of Wiesel as "The Jeremiah of the Holocaust as seen in Jewish isolation." This reviewer has the rather singular view that Wiesel does not concern himself with the liberation of non-Jews.

B29 Fournier, Marie-Jose. "Un Mysticisme Harcelant." Tribune Juive (Paris), No. 192 (March 3-9, 1972), p. 13.
An essay in an issue devoted to Wiesel (see B80).

B30 Friedman, Maurice. "Elie Wiesel: The Modern Job." Commonweal, LXXXV (October 1966), 48-52. Collected in B 5.
A very comprehensive essay review. Mr. Friedman defines the modern Job as: "one who affirms what confronts him as 'the given' of his own existence and at the same time contends with it." He feels that the modern Job begins with the Nazi occupation of France. He traces this theme through Camus' The Plague and the writing of Martin Buber. "The most impassioned complaint, the most stubborn and faithful dialogue with the absurd, the most moving embodiment of the Modern Job is the work of the young writer Elie Wiesel." He discusses this theme through Night, The Accident, Town Beyond the Wall, and Gates of the Forest.

B30a Garber, Frederick. "The Art of Elie Wiesel," Judaism, XXII (Summer 1973), 301-308.
A scathing attack on Wiesel's view of the witness, as seen by Mr. Garber as "tossed out of moral time, loosed from all relations with value, or at least, shuddering at those relations that are left." An indepth essay review covering all the books from Night through O.G.A. After his analysis of the Wiesel canon, Mr. Garber concludes: "however impressive his fervent struggle for form, Wiesel's talent is an insufficient one,

not nearly the sustained voice which the camps have needed.... We ought not to confuse a hungry quest for mode with imaginative accomplishment." [Must reading for those looking for negative material on Wiesel.] See also Judaism, XXIII (Winter 1974), 126, letter to the editor, by Lily Edelman and Mr. Garber's response.

B31 Goldstein, Lawrence. "Survivor's Heritage: The Novels of Elie Wiesel." The Nation, CCIII (October 17, 1966), 390-392.

"The art of Elie Wiesel is shaped by necessity to assert in myth the substance of man's perishable triumphs.... He has dredged from the horror of the Holocaust a vision of man as moving as his suffering and as powerful as his survival."

B32 Halperin, Irving. "Postscript to Death." Commonweal, LXXIX (March 13, 1964), 713-715.

Review-essay of Night, Dawn, The Accident. Theme of all three: "the anguish of a survivor who is unable to exorcise the past or live with lucidity or grace in the present."

B33 _______. "Holocaust Writers and the Critics." Jewish Life, XXXIV (May/June 1967), 19-22.

Mr. Halperin attacks critics who, when reviewing holocaust literature, say the horrors of World War II should be described "obliquely, dryly, cleverly, and above all, coolly."

Of the author, he says that he along with Josef Bor are important writers not by the rules of contemporary fiction but "because they excite the reader to intense reflection."

B34 _______. Jewish Heritage, X (Spring 1968), 5-10 [9-10].

In a book review of Albert H. Friedlander's Out of the Whirlwind, Halperin cites similarities in Wiesel's writings.

B35 _______. "On the Writing and Reading of Holocaust Literature." Jewish Heritage, X (Spring 1968), 40-44.

Wiesel along with the other writers of Holocaust literature find that they must remember and speak out and by extension, the reader is asked to also.

B36 ________. "Meaning and Despair in the Literature of the Survivors." Jewish Book Annual, XXVII. New York: Jewish Book Council of America, 1968, 7-22 [8-9, 19-29].

The section on Wiesel deals with Night. Halperin discusses the personal narrative as an eye witness account of the Jewish tragedy. He also discusses Eugene Heimler's Night of the Mist, Primo Levi's If This Is a Man, and Victor Frankl's From Death Camp to Existentialism.

B37 ________. "Suffering and Fervor in Wiesel's Gates of the Forest." Jewish Book Annual, XXVII. New York: Jewish Book Council of America, 1969, 56-61.

Review essay focusing on themes in Gates of the Forest.

B38 ________. "On Stepping Into the Fiery Gates." Judaism, XXI (Fall 1972), 405-408.

Concerned with Night and Primo Levi's If This Is a Man, twenty-five years later. The lesson learned is the necessity to remain human.

B39 Halperin, Jean. "Un Messager du Passé et de l'Avenir." Tribune Juive (Paris), No. 192 (March 3-9, 1972), p. 12.

An essay appearing in an issue on Wiesel (see B80).

B40 Haymann, Emmanuel. "Elie Wiesel Témoin de la Nuit." Tribune Juive (Paris), No. 192 (March 3-9, 1972), p. 10-11.

An essay appearing in an issue on Wiesel (see B80).

B41 Host, Gerd. "Tilde Unge." Aftenposten (Oslo, Norway), September 16, 1972.

A biographical information sketch.

B42 Hyams, Barry. "Witness and Messenger." The Reconstructionist, XXXII (October 28, 1966), 15-20.

Biographical review-essay of more than ordinary scope. It covers the topics: (1) the death sentence is carried out; (2) baggage of guilt--a heavy burden; (3) the silent spectator; (4) Kaddish; (5) conscience of our time; (6) spiritual crisis in the State of Israel; (7) faith's last stand; (8) does Judaism have the answer; (9) to bear witness. Mr. Hyams concludes with, "Wiesel does not assume the role of judge in his writing. He too is a link.

The key words in his writing are witness and messenger."

B43 Kahn, Lothar. "What Price Jewish Bravery?" The Reconstructionist, XXVIII (June 29, 1962), 14-18.
Dawn is spoken of in an essay-review along with Exodus by Leon Uris.

B44 _______. "Elie Wiesel: Messenger of the Dead." Chicago Jewish Forum, XXIII (Summer 1965), 292-297. Collected in B 7 (altered).
The effect of Hasidism on Wiesel's life is discussed in this essay. Kahn calls Wiesel "the brightest young hope on the Jewish literary horizon."

B45 _______. "The Road to Recovery." Jewish Affairs (Johannesburg), XXI (March 1966), 20-23.
An in-depth essay on the first five books. The question is posed concerning the possibility of Wiesel becoming a great novelist. Mr. Kahn says there is doubt there; but, "as the most powerful spokesman for the survivors of the tragedy, as a prophet, as a re-interpreter of Jewish life through fiction, Wiesel today has no equal on the several continents of this earth."

B46 _______. "French-Jewish Writers: An Overview." Jewish Book Annual, XXV. New York: Jewish Book Council of America, 1967-1968, 60-69 [64-65].
A review of contemporary French-Jewish writers. Wiesel is referred to as a "Jewish Camus" who, having accepted the absurdity of existence, seeks to triumph over it through a modern Hasidic affirmation of joy.

B47 Kaplan, Louis L. "Elie Wiesel: Maker of Legends." Jewish Heritage, VIII (Spring 1966), 20-26. Reprinted (condensed) Jewish Digest, XII (Spring 1967), 51-56.
Presentation address by Louis L. Kaplan to Elie Wiesel, recipient of 1966 Jewish Heritage award for excellence in Literature, containing (1) a biographical and analytical review of the material in Dawn, The Accident, Town Beyond the Wall; (2) an encomium to Mr. Wiesel.

B48 Kaplan, Mordechai M. "Israel, the Jewish People, and the World." The Reconstructionist, XXXIV (February 9, 1968), 16-20.

A Reconstructionist symposium where Wiesel's ideas on the Holocaust are used as a reference point. Wiesel has rightly been termed the conscience of contemporary world Jewry, Kaplan stated.

B49 Korey, William. "The Not So Silent Soviet Jews." New York Times, January 22, 1971, p. L-39.
In an editorial comment, Mr. Korey compares the Silent Jews that Elie Wiesel spoke of a half-decade ago "who only spoke with their eyes" with the young Jewish Soviet Maccabees of today.

B50 Lerner, Max. "The Guilty." New York Post, June 24, 1963, p. 27.
Night is used to focus on the difficulties in the world situation. Mr. Lerner says that the book "will do as well as any to approach some of the problems that later grew out of the Eichmann case. For the Jews were concerned with the problem of historic justice, yet in facing this problem they had to carry along with them a heavy burden of guilt for not having fought back hard enough before and during the concentration camps."

B51 Lovsky, F. "Elie Wiesel: Compagnon des Morts d'Israel." Foi et Vie (Paris), LXVII (January-April 1968), 36-58.
A comprehensive essay-review.

B52 Luckens, Michael J. "Reaction to a Meeting with Elie Wiesel." Judaism, XX (September 1971), 365-368.
Essay-review of The Gates of the Forest, Legends of Our Time, Town Beyond the Wall, and One Generation After.
His meeting with Wiesel was the culmination of a two year relationship with a modern day prophet.

B53 Mandel, Arnold. "Elie Wiesel: Un Ecrivain Significatif." L'Information d'Israel (Paris), May 22, 1964, p. 6.
A French essay.

B54 Maron, Sam. "Elie Wiesel in the Oral Tradition: His Works are Tales, Not Novels." Jewish Exponent, CXLVI (December 5, 1969), 29.
A discussion of the meaning of writing in the oral tradition. Wiesel is called "a modern storyteller in the oral tradition." This review-essay appeared in

connection with a lecture by Wiesel at Temple University.

B55 Mauriac, François. "Un Enfant Juif." Le Figaro Littéraire, No. 633 (June 7, 1958), pp. 1, 4.
A reprint of the preface that appears in Wiesel's La Nuit. Reprinted: Canadian Jewish News, September 21, 1962, pp. 3, 11 [in English]; Morgenbladet (Oslo), August 12, 1972, p. 4 [in Norwegian].

B56 _______. "Le Bloc-Notes de François Mauriac." Le Figaro Littéraire, No. 894 (June 8, 1963), p. 20.
Much comment on his friend, Elie Wiesel and his four books to date: La Nuit, L'Aube, La Jour, La Ville de la Chance.

B57 Meyskah, Line. "Leur Passé Nous Fait Peur." Tribune Juive (Paris), No. 192 (March 3-9, 1972), pp. 14-15.
An essay in an issue largely devoted to Wiesel (See B80).

B58 "Nyttarskveldi i Auschwitz." Morgenbladet (Oslo), October 1, 1970, p. 3.
Biographical and essay material appear in this Norwegian account.

B59 Palmieri, Franco. "Una Sconcertante Testimonianza Ebraica sul Dopo, delle Persecuzioni Naziste." Avanti (Rome), September 11, 1968, p. 3.
An Italian review-essay.

B60 Panim al Panim (New York), No. 99 (March 24, 1961), p. 14.
A Hebrew essay appearing in a New York based publication early in Wiesel's career.

B61 Pawel, Ernest. "Fiction of the Holocaust." Midstream, XVI (June/July 1970), 14-26 [19-20].
The reviewer feels that Wiesel is currently forced into a prophet role, a position he did not seek. He also feels that this position has adversely affected Wiesel's writing. "In Beggar in Jerusalem, the voice of the authentic Godseeker and witness has for some time now been amplified out of all proportion to its natural range."

B62 Politi, Morris. "Chol Aud Yihiu Anashim Yihiye Gam Ha Mashoich." Yidiot Achronot (Tel Aviv), November 13, 1964, Yamin Section, p. 9.
Messianic concepts in connection with Wiesel's work are discussed in this Israeli newspaper account.

B63 Revah, M. Pierre. "Un Grand Conteur Hassidique Parmi Nous: Elie Wiesel." L'Arche, No. 34 (February 25-March 25, 1972), pp. 15-17.
A biographical essay in this Paris based journal of Jewish interest.

B64 Riemer, Jack. "Elie Wiesel: Messenger of the Dead." The Jewish Advocate (Boston), May 19, 1966, Sec. 2, p. 3.
The Job theme is stressed. In this connection the reviewer states that very few people have the power to speak about the holocaust--Wiesel can. "The great artist says one thing a thousand times and Wiesel does this for our generation."

B65 Roditi, E. "Recent Jewish Writing in France." Judaism, XVI (Fall 1967), 485-489 [485].
Wiesel is cited as one of the few serious writers of stature writing in his genre in France.

B66 Roth, John K. "Tears and Elie Wiesel." The Princeton Seminary Bulletin, LXV (December 1972), 42-48.
The reviewer, a member of the Philosophy Department at Claremont Men's College, presents a fascinating perspective from which to view Wiesel's work. From a Christian vantage point he compares God's weeping and man's. He says that his faith in Jesus is encouraged by reading Wiesel.

B67 Rutgers Daily Targum (Rutgers University), December 3, 1970, pp. 5-8.
Special issue on Elie Wiesel to publicize his coming visit to the University; (1) two critiques are included giving two views of Wiesel: "Dialogue of Silence" and "Archivist or Activist"; (2) a review of Beggar in Jerusalem entitled "Under Two Shadows Now"; (3) an interview "Meeting with a Modern Job." Wiesel reiterates his desire to be just a story-teller.

B68 Saal, Rollene W. "Pick of the Paperbacks." Saturday Review, LIII (September 26, 1970), 32.

A fresh look at Wiesel's work that appears in Avon paperbacks. There is much comment on the author and his effect on world youth. "For today's youth, a generation unborn when Europe's fires blazed, Wiesel has illuminated not only the past but the future. That, of course, is his great achievement."

B69 Sanders, Ronald. "La Condition Juive." Midstream, XV (February 1969), 63-68.
Wiesel is referred to as the most stable of Jewish writers today writing in French on the Holocaust.

B70 Schwartzchild, S. "Toward Jewish Unity." Judaism, XV (Spring 1966), 57.
A symposium. Mr. Schwartzchild makes a comment about a gathering in Quebec, Ontario, the previous summer where "the de facto High Priest of our generation turned out to be Elie Wiesel."

B71 Shamir, Shlomo. "Elie Visel Aino Maspik Pitronut." Ha-Aretz (Tel Aviv), December 12, 1971, p. 14.
An essay review in Hebrew, noting Wiesel's nomination for the Nobel Peace Prize. Reprinted: "Irgun Oilaih," Maramrossziget (Tel Aviv), February 1972, p. 3.

B72 Shaviv, Elie. "Hatrahshot V'Payrusha." Masha, July 10, 1964, p. 1-2.
A Hebrew essay covering writing to date.

B73 Sherwin, B. L. "Elie Wiesel and Jewish Theology." Judaism, XVIII (Winter 1969), 39-52.
Much scholarly Jewish reference is contained in this essay. In the last analysis, Wiesel is thought to be a "hopeful worshipper and not a blasphemer ... a novelist and a Kabbalist."

B74 ________. "Elie Wiesel on Madness." Central Conference of American Rabbis (CCAR), XIX (June 1972), 24-32.
Erudite thesis on definitions of madness, delineation of moral madness, which, in this critic's argument, is the dominating idea in Wiesel's writing. "... for Wiesel, madness is moral madness. It therefore entails remaining human and retaining a concern for others in a world in which the social norm is hate and indifference."

B75 Shulman, Eliahu. "Arum Undzara Farlagon." Oifn Shvel (New York), September-October 1965, pp. 1-2.
A Yiddish essay-review.

B76 "Le Silence Royaume de Verbe." L'Arche (Paris), No. 160 (July 1970), p. 67.
A French essay-review in a publication of Jewish interest.

B77 Simon, Pierre-Henri. "L'Oeuvre D'Elie Wiesel: Prix Rivarol." Le Monde, June 19, 1963, p. 11.
A review of the books to date in connection with the winning of the Prix Rivarol.

B78 Steiner, George. "Postscript to a Tragedy." Encounter, XXVIII (February 1967), 33-39 [37, 39].
Wiesel reviewed along with other authors who are survivors of the Holocaust. The reviewer states "only those who actually passed through hell can have the right to forgive. We do not have that right."

B79 Straus, Leonard K. "Jerusalem: A Poem for Elie Wiesel." Conservative Judaism, XXV (Winter, 1971), 58.
A short poem in honor of Elie Wiesel. It contains remembrances contained in Jerusalem of (Wiesel's) parents and past.

B80 "Le Témoignage d'Elie Wiesel: Un Dossier." Tribune Juive (Paris), No. 192 (March 3-9, 1972), pp. 9-19.
The issue is mainly devoted to Wiesel. Individual articles are listed in this section by author. This tribute includes review articles, biographical material, an interview, and many glossy photos.

B81 Ticktin, Harold. "Thinking of the Unthinkable." The American Zionist, LXII (January 1972), 37, 40.
In a review of Irving Halperin's Messengers From the Dead, this critic discusses Halperin's treatment of Wiesel. "His [Halperin's] view of Wiesel as a man who lost his God and seeks a 'Gate' from which he may emerge unscathed is probably the best discussion of Wiesel's mystical works in English."

B82 Wallace, Andrew. "Wiesel Makes Holocaust Meaningful to Youths." Philadelphia Inquirer, October 16, 1971, Sec. 4, p. 4.

A biographical sketch dealing with Wiesel's interest in youth.

B83 Weiss-Rosmarin, Trude. "The Editor's Pages." Jewish Spectator, XXXIII (November 1968), 2, 32.
An overall look at Wiesel in connection with the 25th Anniversary of the Warsaw Ghetto Revolt. Legends of Our Time is especially noted in this regard "because it haunts the reader and forces him to remember."

B84 _______. "The Quality of Jewish Life." Jewish Spectator, XXXVII (January 1972), 2-6 [4].
Mrs. Weiss-Rosmarin states that it is a shame to waste Elie Wiesel's talks on tired Jewish convention audiences. "He should speak before Jewish children story hours."

B85 _______. "Hasidism: Authentic and Inauthentic." Jewish Spectator, XXXVII (April 1972), 7-8.
In editorial comments covering the areas of Israel, the diaspora and Zionism, Mrs. Weiss-Rosmarin focuses on Wiesel's purpose, which she finds is to transmit and not to innovate. "Wiesel's language is direct and sparse. It has that simplicity which is the distinguishing mark of all great writing." She places it in perspective with other writing on Hasidism.

B86 "The Wiesel Phenomenon." Jewish Observer and Mid-East Review (London), XVIII (February 28, 1969), 10.
A review of a talk Wiesel gave at the Bergen-Belsen Association in London. His remarks on the Holocaust were not depressing. "He conveys a kind of mystic joy."

B87 Wyschogrod, Michael. "Faith and the Holocaust." Judaism, XX (Spring 1971), 286-294 [286].
A review-essay of Emil Fackenheim's book, God's Presence in History. Much mention is made of Wiesel's place in the world of holocaust thinkers.

B88 Ziegler, Jean. "Elie Wiesel Qui Fut Cet Enfant Juif." Journal de Génève, No. 168 (July 20-21, 1963), p. 6.
An article dealing with Wiesel's work and the winning of the Prix Rivarol.

B89 _______. "Elie Wiesel: Un Prophète Inquiétant." Coopération (Suisse), No. 46 (November 14, 1964).
A biographical essay.

PERIODICALS--Interviews

B90 Agmon, Yaacov. "Elie Wiesel's Fears." Israel, II (April 1970), 54-55.
This interview appeared originally on Israel Radio "Personal Questions" in Hebrew. It is excerpted here in English translation. Questioned why he doesn't live in Israel, Wiesel replied, "Israel and the Holocaust are two worlds which negate one another." He fears that the world may more and more hold Jews responsible for all the evil in the world.

B91 Bang, Holmboe Erna. "Enjode om Sitt Folk." Morgenbladet (Oslo), January 24, 1969, pp. 3-4.
An interview with biographical information in a Norwegian newspaper.

B92 Baras, Barbara M. Young Israel. Viewpoint, XII (April 29, 1971), 13.
An interview in connection with the 92nd St. "Y" lectures.

B93 Bortoli, Georges. "Elie Wiesel à Vu Dieu Mourir à Buchenwald." Le Figaro Littéraire, June 15, 1963, p. 2.
A French interview.

B94 Brin, Herb. "Wiesel's Warning: Last Chance to Save Jews." Los Angeles Heritage and Southwest Jewish Press, February 25, 1972, pp. 1, 6.
A book review of Souls on Fire is combined with interview comments on the book and the plight of Soviet Jews. He quotes Wiesel in the interview: "If the Jews of Russia feel that we have abandoned them and have failed them, I am convinced that they will try to commit mass cultural suicide.... We have lost enough."

B95 *Drouvet, Jacques-Paul. "Cinq Minutes avec Elie Wiesel: Lauréat du Prix Rivarol." Se Maine Provence, July 7, 1973.
An interview after Wiesel won the Prix Rivarol.

B95a Edelman, Lily. "A Conversation with Elie Wiesel." National Jewish Monthly, LXXXVIII (November 1973), 5-15.
Mrs. Edelman uses this interview to give Wiesel an opportunity to express his views on the October Mid-

East War, American Jewry, and to comment on The Oath. The War: "When the enemy attacked on Yom Kippur, their target was not only Israel but all Jews." The need for the interdependency of Jews is stressed here. The author's comments on the future of the American Jewish Community are somewhat pessimistic. He feels that the moral reserve and spiritual and intellectual baggage that is necessary for survival is lacking. The task of the American Jewish author in this bleak scene is (1) to transmit the Jewish tale and (2) to link universal history to Jewish history. On The Oath: Moshe is the mystery of the tale, the mystic, the poet. Madness is a force for evil as well as good. Wiesel refers here to his concept of mystical or moral madness, not the clinical variety. He sees The Oath as a continuation of T.B.T.W. In that book Michael finds that to save himself is to save another madman--he does this with the deaf-mute in the prison cell. In The Oath, Moshe the madman wants to save the whole world. When he realizes that he can't he wants at least to save his wife. The old man Azriel eventually breaks the silence because he becomes interested in the young man, and that is what saves him. Wiesel believes that to break alienation one must give to receive.

B96 Eckman, Fern Marja. "Out of the Inferno." New York Post, December 10, 1968, Magazine, p. 55.

In an interview after the award of the Prix Medicis, the reviewer finds the author pleased but not jubilant. He states, "the important thing is not to lie, not to become a comedian, not to give a performance, not to be too silent or too talkative, but to have a blank page and fill this in with the right things." Wiesel goes on to comment on the witness theme. A Catholic friend asked why he is still haunted by concentration camps. "I told him, you amaze me. One Jew died 2000 years ago, and you don't stop talking about it. Six million Jews died only 20 years ago. And you want me to forget?"

B97 ________. "Eternal Jew." New York Post, April 28, 1972, "Daily Closeup Magazine," p. 3.

An interview prior to the serialization of Souls on Fire in the New York Post. Background material, personal biographical information, and ideas from the book are given. The reviewer reflects on an occasion when

Wiesel was asked where he felt most at home. He replied, "In Jerusalem--when I am not in Jerusalem."

B 98 *"Elie Wiesel Parlé de la Souffrance d'Israel." Journal des Communautés, No. 419 (June 28, 1968).
A French interview.

B 99 "Entretien avec Elie Wiesel." Aviv (Toulouse), No. 16 (January 1969), p. 1-3.
A lengthy French interview.

B100 "Entretien avec Elie Wiesel." Tribune Juive (Paris), No. 192 (March 3-9, 1972), pp. 16-19.
An editorial staff interview with Mr. Wiesel (see B80).

B101 Flender, Harold. "Conversation with Elie Wiesel." Womens' American Ort Reporter, March/April 1970, p. 4-5.
A penetrating well written interview that gives much valuable insight on Wiesel as a writer, his literary interests, concerns for the world, pessimism and reasons for writing in French.

B102 Fiske, Edward B. "Elie Wiesel: Archivist with a Mission." New York Times, January 31, 1973, pp. 43, 64.
A most comprehensive encomium to Wiesel. Biographical information is updated to include information on Wiesel's marriage and the birth of his son. Popularity as a lecturer is made much of, his position within the American Jewish community is delineated with much documentation of adulatory comments by the rabbinate and others. Rabbi Eugene Borowitz: "He is the closest thing we have in the Jewish community to a superstar." The reviewer says that his research into why the novelist has found responsive chords in virtually every element of the Jewish community has produced the most common reply of "he comes across as authentic," that he has managed to blend his person and his ideas into a single charismatic presence. Reprinted: "Elie Wiesel: The Jewish Superstar." International Herald Tribune (Paris), February 2, 1973, p. 14 (abridged); Rhode Island Herald (Providence), February 9, 1973, pp. 13, 15.

B103 Harpur, Tom. "A Survivor of Auschwitz Asks Why

God Permits Suffering." Toronto Star, October 30, 1971, p. 9.

In a discussion of Wiesel's Hasidic and Orthodox background, this reviewer quotes the author as saying, "This was the environment of my early days and in spite of everything, I still feel closest to it."

B104 Hendrick, Kimmis. "The Whisper That Is a Call." Christian Science Monitor, May 18, 1970, Magazine, p. 8.

The reviewer was concerned about the differences that exist between himself and the author prior to the interview: he discovered how comfortable a person Wiesel is to talk to. He concerns himself with "the whisper that is hope" in Wiesel's writing. Much material on Beggar in Jerusalem.

B105 Houston, Gary. "Profile of a 'Haunted' Writer." Chicago Sun-Times, November 29, 1970, Book Week, p. 16.

Biographical-interview sketch. The reviewer says that Wiesel's vision is of a world "in which the consciousness of any of its constituents--of an individual or of an entire ethnic group and all its ancestors--in time becomes one with the consciousness of the world."

B106 Jardin, Claudine. "Pour Elie Wiesel l'Homme Est Devenu Juif." Le Figaro, No. 6744 (June 9, 1966), p. 23.

B107 Kernan, Michael. "A Survivor." Washington Post, February 6, 1970, B1, B12.

Reprinted: *Springfield (Mass.) Republican, February 22, 1970; Houston Chronicle, March 1, 1970, p. 16; *Staten Island Advance, March 16, 1970; Louisville Courier-Journal Times, March 22, 1970, Sec. F, p. 4.

Much biographical material is included in this interview. Wiesel comments on how he had to see Eichmann again.

B108 *Lacombe, Lia. "Elie Wiesel: Les Autres Existent Tellement Que Si On Sait les Ecouter, On Peut les Incorporer à Nous." Lettres Française (May 6-22, 1963).

Interview after the Prix Rivarol.

B109 Laporte, Marc. "Elie Wiesel: D'Auschwitz à Hiro-

shima." L'Express, June 6, 1963, p. 34.
An interview after the Prix Rivarol.

B110 Malka, Victor. "Face à Face avec Elie Wiesel: Poète de la Souffrance Juive." Reforme, April 1, 1967, p. 11.
Reprinted: Israelitisches Wochenblatt für die Schweiz, May 24, 1968, p. 45.

B111 *"Ontmoeting met Elie Wiesel in Romi Goldmuntz Centrum." Di Nievwe Gazet (Antwerp), May 22-23, 1971.

B112 Palliser, Michel and Schwarz, Francis. "Une Demi-Heure avec Elie Wiesel." La Vie de Bordeaux, January 11, 1969, pp. 1-2.

B113 Rochmis, Dorothy H. "Elie Wiesel: Chronicler of Echos, Curator of the Museum of Memory." California Jewish Voice, February 18, 1972, p. 12.
An interview in connection with a publicity tour for Souls on Fire. Much comment on the book, Wiesel's personal discipline and his upcoming new books.

B114 Salomon, M. "The Jews of Silence: An Interview with Elie Wiesel." Conservative Judaism, XXI (Spring 1967), 49-53.
Much comment on conditions of Soviet Jewry. Mr. Wiesel feels that there is still hope, "But the crucial question is whether the Jews who live in free countries are worthy of their [Russian Jews'] courage and faith."

B115 Schwartz, George. "Wiesel's Lectures Enrich Jewish Studies." The Campus (Undergraduate newspaper of the City College of New York), November 30, 1972, p. 5.
Interview and comments on Wiesel's appointment as a Distinguished Professor of the City College's Jewish Studies department. Much background information given. Wiesel is quoted: "As a man I am a pessimist, because the machine has taken over.... They are dehumanizing man.... They are indifferent to man's fate.... It is very, very sad. As a Jew, I am an optimist because Jews have the Key to survival. If the world were to listen, we could teach it something."

B116 Scurr, Anne. "Youth Created Awareness of Plight of Soviet Jews, Elie Wiesel says Here." San Francisco Jewish Bulletin, February 18, 1972, pp. 1, 18.

An interview in connection with the following: an appearance in the area, a radio Eternal Light script, and Souls on Fire. Wiesel discusses the problems of Soviet Jews and how youth have pointed the way.

B117 Shamir, Shlomo. "Sicha Rishonah Eim Elie Visel." Hadoar Hebrew Weekly (New York), LI (March 17, 1972), 319-320.

In the first part of a two-part interview, Mr. Shamir traces Wiesel's career, commenting critically on his works. He also notes Wiesel's interest in the Hebrew language and his belief in the future of the Hebrew language in the diaspora.

B118 ________. "Sichah Shniah Eim Elie Visel." Hadoar Hebrew Weekly (New York), LI (April 14, 1972), 344.

The second of two conversations with Elie Wiesel.

B118a Sharp, Christopher. "Wiesel on the Holocaust: America Turned Its Back." Women's Wear Daily, November 7, 1973, p. 34.

A personality profile. Comments on the effects of the Israeli Wars of 1967 and 1973. Ideas on silence explored: "I believe that the greatest poetry comes from words that are coated in silence."

B119 Shear, Natalie P. "Elie Wiesel: A Destiny of His Own." Jewish Week, February 12, 1970, p. 2.

The author hopes he will be remembered for Jews of Silence. Wiesel's comments on Israel: "It is a sentimental and emotional experience for me.... I have no fear at all.... Exile is an element of literature and creativity, ... but I cannot work in Israel for there is no need for it. You are there and that is all that is necessary."

B120 Shenker, Israel. "The Concerns of Elie Wiesel: Today and Yesterday." New York Times, February 10, 1970, p. 48.

An interview with Wiesel before the publication of Entre Deux Soleils. Wiesel says "Our generation is the link between the Holocaust and Israel. Like Job we are cursed and haunted by what has happened to us, but--like Job--privileged because it has happened to us." On his recent concern with Hasidic masters, "I try to show that Judaism is not only a philosophy with ethical values, but that a certain Mendele Kotzk is greater than Kierkegaard, and that Rabbi Natan of Bratislava is greater than Kafka."

B121 Srouji, Jacque. "Writer Wishes Only to Reach Individuals." Nashville Tennessean, March 1, 1970, Sec. F, p. 13.
An interview with Wiesel in connection with the author's visit and lecture in Nashville.

B122 Stuttaford, Genevieve. "Souls on Fire: Tales of Hassidism." San Francisco Examiner and Chronicle, February 27, 1972, This World Section, p. 35.
An interview and review of Souls on Fire. Mr. Wiesel makes comments on the Russian poet Yevtushenko, and on the growth of Hasidism: "There is a renaissance of Hasidism especially among the young."

B123 Wershba, Joseph. "An Author Asks Why the World Let Hitler Do It." New York Post, October 2, 1961, p. 30.
Biographical interview. The author comments and answers questions on Eichmann, Hitler and the contention that Jews went to their death passively. "There was resistance in the camps but mainly along political lines. If, in the end, the Jews accepted death, it was their only way of protest. What could they do when the whole world had forgotten them?"

REVIEWS OF BOOKS by Wiesel--English Editions

NIGHT

B124 Alexander, Holmes. "Of Apathy and Duplicity, and the Ultimate Degradation." Tampa Tribune, October 30, 1960, p. 23-A.
Reviewed together with William L. Shirer's The Rise and Fall of the Third Reich. "Some victims of Hitler lost more than their lives. They are the ultimate testimony of Nazi degradation."

B125 Angoff, Charles. "Child at Auschwitz." Philadelphia Jewish Exponent, October 7, 1960, p. 69.
Mankind can profit from reading and rereading Night the reviewer feels, because then "they will never forget the latent bestiality of man." He quotes much from the book and also from Mauriac's preface. Mauriac feels that the book must show the world what Race really is--"the most voracious of all idols."

B126 "Auschwitz Survivor." Cedar Rapids (Iowa) Gazette, October 16, 1960, Sec. 3, p. 8.
"This shocking story should be required reading for anyone who has ever felt that perhaps Hitler's inhumanity toward European Jewry is exaggerated."

B127 Bannon, Barbara. "Forecast of Paperbacks." Publishers' Weekly, CLXXX (November 6, 1961), 46.
A preview of the Pyramid paperback. "The story is almost too harrowing to bear, but the quality of the writing is superb."

B128 Belanger, Bill. "Easier Read Than it is to Forget." Huntington (W. Va.) Herald Advertiser, November 6, 1960, Sec. 3, p. 35.
"It is a must to remind people that what once happened can happen again."

B129 Cade, Elizabeth. "Faith Is Crushed by Concentration Camp Horrors." Philadelphia Inquirer, September 18, 1960, Sec. D, p. 8.
"Elie Wiesel's novel is a penetrating psychological study besides being a dramatic account of true events."

B130 Carr, William B. "German Recalls a Youth Spent in Death Camps." Sacramento Bee, November 27, 1960, p. 11.
Much mention is made of Wiesel's youth. "Through one boy's eyes, it is the story of the attempted murder of a race. It cannot easily be forgotten."

B131 *Cornell, James C. "Why Hast Thou Forsaken Me." Worcester (Mass.) Telegraph, October 23, 1960.
The book is seen as a rite du passage for the author.

B132 Deutch, Howard. Los Angeles Voice, June 16, 1961, p. 4.

The reviewer speaks of all those who were killed in Auschwitz. "The strongest of them do not survive, but Elie Wiesel remains as the remnant of his family, a bookful of memories stored in his brain. He is one who makes the ignominy of the Germans go down in history, a remnant of the persecuted."

B133 Duchavni, Moshe. "A Vehy Geshri fun a Idish Kind be de Floman fun Gas-Oyvan." The Day-Jewish Journal (New York), September 25, 1960, p. 6. Yiddish review of Night.

B133a English Journal, LXIII (January 1974), 49. In a bibliography of "Multi-Ethnic Literature in America," Night is listed in the Jewish-American section, and is termed "a classic among books dealing with the holocaust."

B134 Finn, James. "Terribly Alone in a World Without God." Commonweal, LXXIII (January 6, 1961), 391-392.

The reviewer comments favorably on Mauriac's introduction. He reviews the historic events, and speaks of the dark depths to which the human spirit plummeted, and of the spiritual suffering and sacrifice that cannot be measured. He talks also about Wiesel's Job-like accusations.

B135 de Ford, Miriam Allen. "His God Was Found Wanting." The Humanist, XXI (March/April 1961), p. 122.

Comparison is made with other child diaries like the one by Anne Frank. The reviewer feels that this book carries a profound meaning for Humanists.

B136 *"French Best Seller." Buffalo Courier Express, September 4, 1960.

Mention of Mauriac introduction is made in a mainly descriptive review.

B137 *Gazette (Berkeley, Calif.), January 14, 1961.

Mauriac's preface is cited in this descriptive review.

B138 Greenberg, Joel. "Long Night of Horror." Sydney Morning Herald (Australia), February 18, 1961, p. 13.

A comprehensive review, containing many plaudits for Wiesel: "an auspicious debut"; "Stella Rodway's translation is beyond praise"; "*Night* ought to become a standard text on this most melancholy subject."

B139 Gros, Charles G. *The Critic*, XIX (November 1960), 44.
This reviewer states that he shares Mauriac's conviction that *Night* should have as many readers as did *The Diary of Anne Frank*.

B140 Grusd, Edward E. *National Jewish Monthly*, LXXV (January 1961), 43.
"Wiesel harrows the reader's soul and makes one understand how the sensitive, religious, mystical youth came to hate the very God he had once loved with such all-consuming passion."

B141 Harer, Wesley H. *Christian Century*, LXXVIII (January 18, 1961), p. 84.
"This book should be given a place beside Anne Frank's diary as a personal record of a child's experience of the Jews during the persecution of the Nazis." An unforgettable moment that is singled out: the Polish Juliek plays Beethoven among the corpses.

B142 Haile, Vera. "A Simple Case of Persecution." *San Francisco Examiner*, January 22, 1961, "Highlight" Sec., p. 8.
"*Night* is the finest story of the effect of Jewish persecution I have read." The reviewer feels that there is no emotionalism or self-pity exhibited. "It is intensely personal, yet beyond blame and melodrama."

B143 Healey, Robert C. "A World Without Love or Mercy." *New York Herald Tribune*, January 1, 1961, p. 28.
"No superfluous flesh on this gaunt and powerful narrative."

B144 Heimler, Eugene. "Funeral of Faith." *London Jewish Chronicle*, September 16, 1960, p. 17.
A review of the British edition. Reviewed together with David Karp's *The Sleepwalkers*. "This is the story of the child whose inner world was killed before it had time to grow into fruition."

B145 "Hinweise." New York Aufbau, January 6, 1961, p. 17.
German review of Night.

B146 "Horror Reality." Sacramento Union, November 6, 1960, p. 7-A.
Much mention is made of Mauriac's preface, much quoting from book.

B147 "Individual Loss." Times Literary Supplement (London), August 19, 1960), p. 523.
A discussion of the suffering the author endured.

B148 Ivry, Itzhak. "Memory of Torment." Saturday Review, XLIII (December 17, 1960), 23-24.
Because of Wiesel's personal experiences he has the unique quality of having been "a child in Hell." Informative material on the Joint Distribution Committee and Braichah is presented.

B149 *"Jewish Victims of the Nazis." Hawkes Bay (Eng.) Herald Tribune, May 11, 1960.
"Wiesel helps us understand the extent of the Nazi tyranny, the enormity of the pillage and racial murder carried out in its name, and the degradation and anguish it inflicted on millions of Jewish people forced to exist under the most horrible conditions--and this the 20th Century."

B150 Jones, Carter Brooke. "Barbarity is Theme of Wartime Document." Washington Star, November 13, 1960, p. C5.
"Of all the documentary narratives of barbarity and suffering which have come out of World War II, none is more poignant than this brief account."

B151 Kazin, Alfred. "The Least of These." The Reporter, XXIII (October 27, 1960), 54-57. Collected in his Contemporaries, B8.
An in-depth review containing comments on Mauriac's introduction, the Job-like accusations that unite Wiesel with the religion of his fathers. "I don't think that I shall soon forget the picture of this young boy standing on a mound of corpses, accusing God of deserting His creation."

B152 Kirkus, XXVII (August 1, 1960), 660.

A comparison with Anne Frank's diary is made. "There is no spiritual or emotional legacy here to offset any reader reluctance."

B153 Leeper, Clare d'Artois. "True Story of One Who Escaped Nazi Death." Baton Rouge Advocate, January 22, 1961, Sec. E, p. 2.

The survival theme of the novel is mentioned, along with its lack of a depressing quality. "While it is disillusioning to accept Night for the true story that it is, it is even more shocking to accept the fact that its narrator belongs not to some primeval past but to the present: for Elie Wiesel is only thirty-five years old!"

B154 Logan, Terry Colangelo. "They Refused to Believe." Chicago Sun Times; November 13, 1960, Sec. 3, p. 3.

Reviewed together with I Was A Spy by Marion Miller. "I found Night a book of beauty and understanding. In spite of all that has been written about the concentration camps, this held interest and sympathy."

B155 *Mail (Oxford, England), July 21, 1960.

Review of British edition. The book is compared to The Diary of Anne Frank. "The horror of Elie Wiesel's story is not in the brutalities committed against the body which he, unlike his mother, sister, and father, survived, but in the violence perpetrated against the mind of a schoolboy."

B156 Maizlich, Ruth. "Speaking of Books." Los Angeles Voice, December 1, 1961, p. 4.

Both Night and Dawn are reviewed here. It is in the peculiar quality of the particular night and the dawn that makes the link between these two books, according to this reviewer.

B157 Meuller, Herbert V. "Recalled After Fifteen Years." Denver Post, September 25, 1960, "Roundup" section, p. 16.

Night is reviewed favorably along with other holocaust books.

B158 *Meyers, Robert R. "Human Depravity Fed on Helplessness." Dallas Times Herald, October 16, 1960.

"In an anguish that is almost tangible, Wiesel opens a small window upon the world of cruelty and desperation. No reader will be able to forget what he sees there."

B159 Michalopoulos, Andre. "Auschwitz Horror Relived in Night." Boston Advertiser, December 20, 1964, p. 45.
A review of the Pyramid paperback. The review speaks of the degradation and brutality civilized man is capable of.

B160 Mindlin, Hilary. "No Single Book Describes the Horror Completely." The Jewish Floridian (Miami), October 21, 1960, p. 14-A.
The first half of the book is described as being "extraordinary." In the second half of the book "the sensitivities of the sufferer become blunted and he cannot convey his suffering adequately."

B161 National Jewish Post, XVI (September 30, 1960), 7.
"Perhaps the finest narrative to derive from the Hitler barbarism."

B162 News Globe (Amarillo, Texas), September 11, 1960, p. 7.
The theme of loss of faith is discussed.

B163 New Yorker, XXVII (March 18, 1961), 175.
The reviewer states that the concentration camp appears to be one of the distinctive institutions of the twentieth century and that Mr. Wiesel's book has conveyed its essence. He goes on to say that M. Mauriac's foreword succinctly states the appalling metaphysical question it poses to the Christian.

B164 Nyren, Dorothy. Library Journal, LXXV (September 1, 1960), 2932.
In a brief review, the theme of "asking the question" is particularly noted. It is recommended by the reviewer.

B165 Ort, Dan. "Concentration Camp Turns Boy, 14 into 'Accuser of God' in Night," Fort Wayne (Ind.) News Sentinel, September 17, 1960, p. 4.
"The book in its journalistic prose carries the theme of persecution and survival. Its sad intensity

makes the reader cry: 'Why can't they let you live?'"

B166 Paull, Irene. "The Night of Nazism." Jewish Currents, XV (April 1961), 39-40.
The reviewer wishes that the book "could be compulsory reading for every German school child."

B167 Potts, Paul. London Magazine, I (April 1961), 91, 93.
The reviewer was very moved by the account of the author's survival. "This book, a factual record, is a human document of the utmost importance." Once again, special note is made of Mauriac's introduction.

B168 Price, Emerson. "Child Victim of Nazis, Now Grown Writes of Bestial Horrors." Cleveland Press, September 20, 1960, "The Press Weekly" section, p. 9.
Comparison made with The Diary of Anne Frank. In discussing the importance of the book the reviewer states: "If the Nazis brutalized themselves, they succeeded also brutalizing--to a large extent--the whole of mankind.... His story is one that must be read by everyone interested in a respectable destiny for the human family."

B169 ________. Cleveland Press, May 30, 1961, p. A-5.
A short descriptive review of the paperback edition.

B170 Rogoff, Hillel. "De Nacht." Jewish Daily Forward (New York) August 28, 1960, Sec. 2, p. 5.
Yiddish review of Night.

B171 Samuels, Gertrude. "When Evil Closed In." New York Times Book Review, November 13, 1960, p. 20.
The review details the events of how Wiesel "who survived the 'night' that destroyed his parents and baby sister, lost his God." It also calls the book "a slim volume of terrifying power ... a Kafka-like madness."

B172 Schweder, William G., S.J. Best Sellers, XX (September 15, 1960), 207.
The Mauriac introduction, the theme of loss of faith, and the idea of beastliness are treated in this review.

B173 Smolar, Boris. "Two on Eichmann." New York Post, October 2, 1960, Magazine Section, p. 11.
Night is reviewed along with Minister of Death: The Adolph Eichmann Story by Quentin Reynolds, Ephriam Katz, Zwy Aldouby.
Mauriac preface noted. Background material on Eichmann given, along with the hope that his trial may help the world learn what has happened to modern man.

B174 ______. "Between You and Me." Canadian Jewish Chronicle, December 23, 1960, p. 4.
Mauriac's preface and Stella Rodway's translation noted in a very favorable review. Reprinted: American Examiner, December 29, 1960, p. 5; Jewish Advocate (Boston), CXXVIII (January 12, 1961), Section 2, p. 3.

B175 Thames, Roger. "Another Look at Horror." Birmingham (Ala.) News, November 6, 1960, p. E-7.
This reviewer talks about his G.I. experiences which include having seen Buchenwald "from a well-fed perspective." He now sees the horror again that he saw there fifteen years ago.

B176 Tucker, Daisy S. "Author's Family Met Death in Flames of Nazi Furnace." Columbus (Ga.) Enquirer, October 3, 1960, p. 13.
Focus is on autobiographical aspects of the book.

B177 "Wiesel Gives Youth's Account of Nazi Terrorism in Night." Detroit Jewish News, September 9, 1960, p. 4.
Appears on editorial page as a feature review. Much mention is made of Mauriac's introduction and the horrors of Hitlerism. "It is a story to be shared with all liberty loving people, so that the tragedy of Nazism should never be forgotten, so that the Hitlerite brutalities may never again be repeated."

DAWN

B178 "An Israeli Recruit's Time of Decision." Detroit News, April 23, 1961, p. 3-G.
Much of the plot is summarized in this review along with analytical comments on the style: "Starkly

written, bare of detail, terrifying in emotional impact, this story builds up to an unbelievably powerful climax."

B179 Angoff, Charles. "Who Guides Human Conduct?" Jewish Exponent (Philadelphia), CXXXI (October 27, 1961), 23.
"Dawn is even better than Night. It is a profound document of our time ... and of the deep dark abysm of human history."

B180 * ________. "Recruited to Avenge Hanging of an Israeli." In Jewish Bookland (February 1962).
"Dawn is filled with wonderful and warm Chassidic lore. It is filled with the special kind of 'atheism' peculiar to certain very devout Jews. There is nothing in contemporary Jewish literature like it, not even remotely like it."

B181 "Anguished Souls." Newsweek, LVII (June 12, 1961), 96.
"Novelist Wiesel writes with a concise clarity--partly the result of tireless effort and partly derived from his sense of the spirit, and spirituality of these matters."

B182 Ball, James, S.J. Best Sellers, XXI (May 15, 1961), 90.
The reviewer calls the book an example of the changed role of Jews in the modern world. "After centuries of passive suffering they are now returning evil for evil." Though he lauds the theme, he finds the style wanting. "The book does not hold you. You are interested in how the action ends, but a glance at the last page solves that. One obstacle to maintaining interest is that there are too many loose ends, throwbacks, explanations. Probably, too, the effort at symbolism hampers the author."

B183 Belanger, Bill. "Theme Old but Novel Well Told." Huntington (W. Va.) Herald Advertiser, July 9, 1961, Sec. 3, p. 33.
A positive portrayal of the novel's themes, characterizations is given.

B184 Berger, Joel S. "Eye for an Eye." Worcester (Mass.) Telegram, May 14, 1961, p. D-9.

Contains good plot summary and plaudits for flashback and stream of consciousness techniques.

B185 Booklist, LVII (March 15, 1961), 450.
A brief descriptive review.

B186 Bookmark, XX (July 1961), 234.
"... the enormity of war and violence is made intensely clear in a memorable short novel."

B187 "Brief Encounter." Times Literary Supplement (London), February 2, 1962, p. 69.
The reviewer feels this is a book of profound quality. "Not a word is wasted; not another word is needed; the whole is the kind of complete achievement which illuminates and in some degree enlarges experience." The portagonist, Elisha, and the British army captain are thought of as each playing a role which has been imposed upon him. "The two roles are extremities of the estate of man, the tragic thing is the imposition."

B188 Christian Century (Chicago), LXXII (July 11, 1962), 866.
Brief descriptive review.

B189 Cole, Thomas L. "A Reluctant Executioner." Chattanooga (Tenn.) Times, July 9, 1961, p. 14.
In a brief descriptive review, the novella is called "a thoughtful serious study, well translated from the French."

B190 Connolly, Brendon. America, CVI (October 21, 1961), 98, 102.
Mr. Connolly feels that the book can be read from the wrong perspective, and he suggests that it be read "as the objective and very skillful plumbing of a decent soul faced with a problem too big for it--and acutely conscious of the fact." If read with this in mind, the reviewer feels the book "will yield a poignant artistic experience."

B191 Devaney, James. "Ghosts of Past." Hartford Courant, May 14, 1961, "Magazine" section, p. 19.
"This is a good tale in a small package."

B192 Feldman, Irving. "After the Death Camps." Com-

mentary, XXXII (September 1961), 262.
The case of Elisha in Dawn in likened to the situation of "God died at Auschwitz," presented in Night.

B193 Fichtner, Margaret Caufield. "Volume Slim but it Packs a Punch." Birmingham (Ala.) News, August 6, 1961, p. E-4.
"The dramatic suspense of this novel and the keen insight upon the heart and mind of a tormented man has seldom been surpassed. It is a terrifying volume, but you won't put it down."

B194 Fleischer, Leonore. "Paperbacks." Publishers Weekly, CXCVI (November 17, 1969), 83.
A preview of the Avon paperback. "A thought provoking book and a very moral one."

B195 Healey, Robert C. "A Moral Man Trapped." New York Herald Tribune Book Review, April 30, 1961, p. 28.
The book is referred to as an eloquent novel. "Within the simple framework of Elisha's soul-searching, which has many cabalistic overtones, Elie Wiesel has provided a moving and suggestive statement of the moral basis for the new Israel."

B196 "Human Despair Explored in Three Bleak but Powerful Novels." Omaha (Neb.) World Herald, August 6, 1961, "Magazine" sec. p. 24.
Dawn is reviewed along with The Pawnbroker by Edward Lewis Wallant and The Arena by William Haggard.
In Dawn, "Mr. Wiesel has taken the stuff of the Jewish underground struggle and turned it into a powerful morality tale. Its inevitability sears the mind as the artistry lifts it."

B197 Kattan, Naim. Montreal Congress Bulletin, June, 1961, p. 3.
The theme of victim as executioner is stressed.

B198 Kirkus, XXIX (February 15, 1961), 177.
Dawn is called a spare spectral novel, dealing with Elisha, the protagonist, facing the fear of becoming a killer. "Perhaps not a popular form or theme, but it leaves an inevitable impress."

B199 Lehrman, Hal. "Israel Under Siege." Saturday Review, XLIV (July 8, 1961), 16.
Mr. Lehrman feels that the past impinges too heavily on the characters in the story. Nevertheless he feels that parts of the book such as the scene in the cellar, "shine gemlike like delicate writing despite interruptions from the omnipresent ghosts."

B200 Levy, Henry W. "To Kill in Cold Blood?" Baltimore Sun, April 30, 1961, Sec. A, p. 5.
The theme of questions with no answers has a universality, according to this review. The conflicts in Laos, Algiers and the Congo bear comparison to the Israeli underground struggle described here.

B201 Light, James F. "A Motley Sextet." Minnesota Review, II (Fall 1961-Summer 1962), 103-110 [106].
Dawn is given kudos in contrast to the other five books reviewed. "Mr. Wiesel implies that the new dawn comes at the expense of the ancient Jewish spirit. About this loss, he seems neither saddened nor joyful; he is only poignantly aware of it."

B203 Mindlin, Hilary. "Slender Fragment of a Much Longer Literary Vision," Miami Jewish Floridian, May 19, 1961, p. 14-A.
This reviewer feels that Wiesel does not expand the problem he poses, which she states as "... the ethics of Sinai pitted against values by power out of pragmatism ... his hero is too much haunted by the ghosts of his past really to grapple with those of his future."

B204 Mitgang, Herbert. "An Eye for an Eye." New York Times Book Review, July 16, 1961, p. 23.
Mr. Mitgang says that Wiesel has built knowledge into artistic fiction. He calls Dawn "a book that hits home at the unsentimental heart, a strong morality tale written from the inside."

B205 Nelson, Floyd W. "Dawn." Sioux Falls (Iowa) Argus-Leader, May 14, 1961, p. 9C.
A mainly descriptive review.

B206 New York Times, April 18, 1961, p. 34.
A descriptive preview of book.

B207 *North DeKalb (Ga.) Record, June 8, 1961.
"Tremendous emotion is evoked from this poignant though bitter tale."

B208 Nyren, Dorothy. Library Journal, LXXXVI (April 1, 1961), 1482.
Dawn is recommended for all collections of superior fiction.

B209 Poling, Daniel A. Christian Herald, August, 1961, p. 50.
"A brilliant book, much in little."

B210 "Terrorist's Act Dramatic Stuff." Lafayette (Ind.) Journal and Courier, May 13, 1961, p. 7.
"A book for mankind, not for a single man."

B211 Wientraub, Benjamin. Chicago Jewish Forum, XIX (Summer 1961), 342-343.
The reviewer feels that the book did not evoke appreciation of Elisha's agony. "Elie Wiesel's book is a gruesome and a racily told story, but nothing more."

B212 "Wiesel's Novel Dawn Traces Irgunist Underworld Actions." Detroit Jewish News, July 21, 1961, p. 4.
Good background information given on Irgun.

B213 Yount, David. "Dawn." The Critic, XIX (July 1961), 24-25.
"Elisha is no tragic hero, he lacks the human dimensions for tragedy. If anything, he is a melodramatic victim, a child caught in the web of circumstance. Elie Wiesel has attempted to make Elisha the Jewish Everyman, forgetting that Everyman is No Man.... Elisha never comes to life sufficiently."

B214 Zyskind, Irvin. "Youth Named Executioner of Officer." Columbus (Ga.) Inquirer, April 24, 1961.
Mainly a plot summary with emphasis on victim as executioner theme.

THE ACCIDENT

B215 "The Accident by Wiesel Adds to Author's Fame." Detroit Jewish News, April 27, 1962, p. 29.

"The Accident is a stirring tale, attesting to the skill of the author as an able narrator."

B216 Angoff, Charles. "Speaking of Books." Philadelphia Jewish Exponent, CXXXII (April 27, 1962), 21.
After retracing the themes of the two previous books, Mr. Angoff calls the present novella "a sort of fictional collage," because it weaves Chassidic lore, comments about the nature of God, reality, and existence into the tale. He says it is not for those who want a book of action, but for those "who want to get close to a memorable retelling of a horror filled, God intoxicated, haunting psychological experience."

B217 *________. "If My Past Is Buried, I Am Buried with It." In Jewish Bookland, October 1962.

B218 Booklist, LVIII (February 16, 1962), 565.
A brief descriptive review.

B219 *Brogneaux, Patricia. "Man's Conscience Probed in Deep Sensitive Tale." Indianapolis Star, March 25, 1961.
"Wiesel's book is a sensitive probing of a man's conscience, his fears and his beliefs. The reader may find himself so involved that he may grow impatient with other members of the story who cannot seem to understand as he [the protagonist] does. Through the barriers of the written word, Wiesel has managed wonderfully to communicate with his readers."

B220 *Crawford, William. "The Accident." El Paso (Texas) Times, May 6, 1962.
"It is neat, clean, precise prose, uncluttered by murky messages, pseudo-profound philosophy or cliches, either in ideal or dialogue.... This novel has every opportunity to be morbid, depressing and disgusting. It is not. It is almost a lyrical prayer."

B221 Finn, James. "A Man Apart." Commonweal, LXXVI (June 22, 1962), 332-333.
The review states that for the Christian not having been faced with the difficulties of the protagonist, accaptance will be difficult, but therein lies a virtue of the book.

B222 First, Helen G. "Curl Up and Read." Seventeen, XXI (May 1962), 84.
"Identification with the suffering living brings Wiesel's Godforsaken and conflicted hero of Night and Dawn to maturity."

B222a Hayman, Jane. "The Accident." Hadassah Magazine, XLII (May 1962), 13.
Moral myths are discussed. Wiesel is said to question man's right to lie to himself. "The Accident is the work of a writer of stature. It is a small work of art, skillfully contrived, which conveys at the same time nightmarish evil and dream-like beauty."

B223 Jacobs, Willis D. New Mexico Quarterly, XXXII (Spring-Summer 1962), 79.
A descriptive review which discusses memory and conscience. It concludes by saying that at the end of the book the young man promises to forget his memories and stifle his conscience, but that he lies.

B224 Kirkus, XXX (January 1, 1962), 30.
The book is said to mix existentialist ethic with the Hassidic hymn. It is "Babel and Singer juxtaposed against Camus and Sartre."

B225 Klare, Gayne. "The Accident." Montreal Canadian Jewish Congress Bulletin, April 1962, pp. 6, 8.
"One can only hope that in any forthcoming novels, Mr. Wiesel may write his fine talent is released from its present elegiac metre."

B226 *Levy, Henry W. "Accident or Suicide." Baltimore Sun, September 2, 1962.
The reviewer calls it not quite as "poignant or challenging as Night or as emotionally or tragically dramatic as Dawn."

B227 *Los Angeles Reporter, October 10, 1962.

B228 "Loss of Will to Live." New York Times, February 26, 1962, p. 24.
A descriptive preview of the book.

B229 Mainord, Ruth. "French Novelist Writes Unusual, Powerful Story." Jackson (Tenn.) Sun, May 27,

1962, p. 9-B.
Calls The Accident "powerful" "sensitive" writing. "It is the writing of a young man--a man who has known horror and despair and can translate them into word pictures. Those who respond to the writing of Albert Camus and François Mauriac will find Wiesel's writing akin to theirs."

B230 *Maizlish, Ruth. Los Angeles Voice, March 30, 1962.
"The Accident reveals the scarred psyche of the survivor of brutalities recounted in the earlier volumes, tortured by his memories to the point where he can no longer bear existence.... The Accident together with its companion volumes Night and Dawn is, in this scribe's view, among the greatest literature that has come out of the terrible holocaust."

B231 Mindlin, Hilary. Miami Jewish Floridian, March 23, 1962, p. 14-A.
The Accident is called the best of the three books to date. "It is a strong book of terrifying vision which spills daylight into the darker rooms of the soul, stirring up all the lust for death." Comparison to Shwartz-Bart's Last of the Just is made. Much mention is made of the psychological wrestling of the inner psyche that occurs in the book. "It is to the poetry of the inner vision that Elie Wiesel gives his tortured obeisance--to the real world which runs like a stream of pain beneath the civilized overlay in every man."

B232 Mitgang, Herbert. "Suspended Between Life and Death." New York Times Book Review, April 15, 1962, p. 36.
Mr. Mitgang feels that the horrors of the past superimposed on a New York setting become falsely melodramatic. He calls the style of this novella "staccato." "Being on the right side does not a novel make."

B233 Norris, Hoke. "Puzzle of Modern Life." Chicago Sun-Times, April 22, 1962, Sec. 3, p. 4.
It is the judgment of this critic that the problem of modern man as stated by Wiesel is how to live in the presence of death. He questions the use of the single individual as a symbol for the condition of man. "Perhaps the survivors of death can console the other

half of humanity that is unaware that it is dying. It is a good puzzle, even if you don't solve it."

B234 Paulding, Gouverneur. "Messenger of the Dead." New York Herald Tribune Books, April 8, 1962, p. 15.
In this review, of what is called a "tersely eloquent book," the reader is said to be compelled to take part in the life-death debate, and to argue as best he can for the value of life.

B235 Pine, John C. Library Journal, LXXXVII (March 1, 1962), 996.
A descriptive review, the book is recommended for all collections.

B236 Price, Emerson. "Exceptional Tale." Cleveland Press, March 27, 1962, Sec. A, p. 6.
In a mainly descriptive account of the work, the review goes on to say: "The book probes anew the haunting despair of those who have seen too much brutality and death."

B237 Ross, Jean. "Alienation." San Francisco People's World, May 12, 1962, p. 7.
It is felt here that the theme of the book is not simply alienation from God, but the much more pressing problem of non-communication.

B238 Smolar, Boris. "Books of Interest." Rochester (N.Y.) Jewish Ledger, May 11, 1962, p. 8.
Mr. Smolar discusses the autobiographical nature of the book. He says that the author is not afraid to die of the accident because he has seen death in crueler forms. "It is extremely well written, establishing Mr. Wiesel as one of the finest authors in contemporary literature."

B239 Stern, Harry J. "A Man's Heroic Struggle to Accept Life." Canadian Jewish Chronicle, May 3, 1963, p. 13.
The key to the importance of the book is the understanding "of the moral problem of the guilt of being alive and the shame of having survived the Nazi holocaust."

B240 Williams, Miller. "A Painful but Never Monotonous

Story." Baton Rouge Advocate, April 1, 1962, p. 2-E.

"Though the book deals with all aspects of suffering, it is painful but never monotonous." There is much comparison to Camus and Richard Yates. "If I knew what a genius is, I would probably call him [Wiesel] one."

THE TOWN BEYOND THE WALL

B241 Adelman, George. Library Journal, LXXXIX (July 1964), 2828.

A descriptive review--the book is highly recommended.

B242 Appel, David. "Haunting Tale of City Pawn in Two Wars." Philadelphia Inquirer, May 31, 1964, Sec. 7, p. 7.

Much detail is given from the book. Wiesel is called a "meticulous prose artisan who is at his most effective in the brief fiction form, larded with legend and haunting questions that beset an ever-questioning man."

B243 Bellman, Samuel I. "The Agony Relived." Congress Bi-Weekly, XXXII (February 1, 1965), 14.

The reviewer says the mood is reminiscent of Kafka at his most depressed and of Samuel Beckett's "end of the world" dialogues. He calls T.B.T.W. moving and utterly absorbing. "A 'black book' neither for the tender-hearted nor for those quick to forgive and make a fast dollar."

B244 Bliven, Naomi. "Valley of the Shadows." New Yorker, XL (January 9, 1965), 115-116.

"There is no doubt that he [Wiesel] writes less to create a fiction then to create a disturbance in the minds of his readers."

B245 Cassill, R. V. "Act of Compulsion." New York Herald Tribune Book Week, June 7, 1964, p. 16.

"Evil is human, weakness is human: indifference is not." The reviewer feels that this precept of Wiesel's fourth book needs to be sought in its detail and form and not merely in thematic epigrams. He develops this idea in a discussion of the passion of the hero, Michael, who he feels is left indifferent to many moral realities.

B246 Elman, Richard M. "Parable of Faith." New Republic, CLI (September 5, 1964), 32-34.
"In T.B.T.W. Wiesel finds both emblem and aesthetic in the Dostoevskyan vision of insanity."

B247 Frankel, Theodore. "Out of Auschwitz--Balm?" Midstream, X (December 1964), 103-106.
Mr. Frankel criticizes Wiesel's portrayal of myth. He feels that the subject of the solution to Auschwitz is too great to handle. "It is so far outside normal experience and so far from the usual categories of thinking and feeling that it cannot be mastered and assimilated."

B248 Friedman, Joseph J. "The Shame of Survival." Saturday Review, XLVII (July 25, 1964), 26.
The reviewer criticizes Wiesel for writing an heroic fantasy. He says that sections in "The Prayer" are rendered diffuse by parables and moralizing passages and that they lack narrative pressure.

B249 Gross, John. New York Review of Books, III (September 10, 1964), 11-12.
Mr. Gross calls the book: "an ambitiously conceived and passionately executed work, which has very considerable merits in its own right." He says that Wiesel's themes would tax the strength of the very greatest artists. He makes comparison to Tolstoy's "accursed questions" where the ultimate mysteries of human existence are dealt with. "What is remarkable is not that he [Wiesel] should sometimes flounder in such tough seas, but what he keeps afloat at all."

B250 Kahn, Lothar. Chicago Jewish Forum, XXIII (Fall 1964), 52-54.
An essay-review of Holocaust literature. T.B.T.W. is reviewed along with Piotr Rawicz's Blood from the Sky and Mendel Mann's At the Gates of Moscow.
Of the three books, Mr. Kahn calls Wiesel's novel a minor masterpiece. He notes the continuing dialogue started in the earlier works, of argument with the Divinity for the injustices and horrors permitted. Wiesel takes that dialogue further in this novel Mr.

Kahn asserts. Here, "it is man's assumption of responsibility for his own actions and his own involvement in the affairs of others which offer the sole hope for his meaningful existence."

B251 Kirkus, XXXII (March 15, 1964), 321.
"The sufferings of the Jews (or of humanity) are introverted here into a picture something like the back-view of one of Chagall's tortured prophets."

B252 Steele, Richard. "Death Stalks Grotesquely Beyond the Wall." Pittsburgh Press, June 7, 1964, Sec. 5, p. 7.
There is much mention of the protagonist, Michael, and of his learning never to desert humanity. This critic feels that of the thousands of books that have been, and will continue to be written about the holocaust, Town Beyond the Wall is one of the best of them "because of its terrible sincerity, its probing quality, its intelligence, and the poetry of its style.... Mr. Wiesel is a writer of very great distinction."

B253 Stern, Daniel. Hadassah Magazine, XLV (June 1964), 20-21.
"Wiesel's fourth novel, Town Beyond the Wall, demonstrates that he has woven a fresh vision of existence out of black despair.... This is a genuine masterpiece. It must be read."

B254 ________. "Suicide, Madness or God?" New York Times Book Review, July 5, 1964, pp. 14-15.
Mr. Stern says that the hero, Michael, weaves the themes of his own alienation into an affirmation of community. "He makes his existential leap--precisely as far as the next human being." He feels that Michael has enacted a legend in which the roles of God and man are reversed. He calls Wiesel's writing a deeply personal, poetic style which has conjured up a painful but healing vision. "Not since Albert Camus has there been such an eloquent spokesman for man."

B255 Time, LXXXII (May 29, 1964), 92.
A brief descriptive review.

B256 Wells, Leon. "In the Shadows of the Past." The Reconstructionist, XXX (November 13, 1964), 28-31.

The reviewer comments on the acclaim writers of the holocaust have received in France. He calls T.B.T.W. one of the masterpieces of this type of literature. "The poetic language and the great philosophic thoughts based on Jewish tradition make this book extraordinary." He feels that Wiesel forces the reader to understand the feelings and reactions of his protagonist, Michael, and hundreds like him who, "carry the dead on their backs." He calls the book an eloquent condemnation of the neutrality of "spectators" throughout the world who did not protest.

B257 "The World's Indifference." Newsweek, LXIII (May 25, 1964), 116, 118.
"It is a legend--archaic, modern, timeless; a legend of an assent from purgatory to possibility."

GATES OF THE FOREST

B258 "Allegory and Anguish." Lincoln (Neb.) Journal and Star, May 29, 1966, p. 15-F.
Much detail is given about the protagonist, Gregor. In-depth critical comment includes the following: "Wiesel has a driving, often extravagent style. He weaves together a surrealistic narrative filled with rugged, disturbing imageries. He thrusts into the reader's ken a sorrowful, ritualistic chant, a primitive cry from age-old decadent Europe for relief from Man's persecution of Man." Reprinted: *Owensboro (Ky.) Messenger-Inquirer, June 13, 1966.

B259 Alter, Robert. "Arraigning God." Book Week, III (May 29, 1966), 2.
The reviewer states that, like Camus, Wiesel's fiction is built around a series of ultimate confrontations. "His [Wiesel's] novels arraign God, question Him, and His ways, struggle to redefine Him, and to recast in the imagination what man's place vis-à-vis God should be."

B260 American Jewish Life. "Book of the Month." May 24, 1966, p. 23.
A positive descriptive review.

B261 Ancrum, Calhoun. "Wiesel Novel Blends Realistic Mystical." Charleston (S.C.) News and Courier, July 3, 1966, p. 5-B.

The style of the book is called at times "almost scriptural, which makes the cruelties it exposes almost unbearable." The discussion is labeled "Talmudic." "From the very first page, one gets an impression of Chassidic ecstasy, even in the face of death and ruin." It is a book that "affects one permanently in one's evaluation of life."

B262 Anderson, LaVere. Tulsa World, June 26, 1966, Your World Mag. Sec., p. 7.
This review credits Wiesel with a remarkable accomplishment: "combining ancient legend, modern horror and the question of lost faith in one anguished narrative. His novel is filled with allegory, religious questioning, exotic peasant scenes, introspective cravings and startling contrasts, all written in a driving prose style."

B263 Baldick, Robert. "A Cataclysm of Grotesques." London Daily Telegraph, February 16, 1967, p. 20.
In a review of the British edition, this critic states that Wiesel's theme--the proper attitude of man in a world God has abandoned--is nobly handled. There is praise for the translation. "This is a novel which aims high, and reaches the mark."

B264 Booklist, LXII (July 1, 1966), 1033.
A brief descriptive review.

B265 *"Both Myth and Realism." Worcester (Mass.) Telegram, May 29, 1966.
The review singles out the lyrics of the book.

B266 Brady, Charles A. "Well Told Stories of God and Israel." Buffalo (N.Y.) News, May 28, 1966, p. B-12.
G.O.T.F. is reviewed along with The Mission by Hans Habe and The God of the Beginnings by Robert Aron. There are large descriptive passages in which the Judas theme and Gavriel as a deaf-mute are cited in detail. "Profound insights glint on every page."

B267 Brietner, Bina. "Speaks as One Dead." Arizona Republic, September 11, 1966, p. C-21.
Concentrates on the theme of Gavriel searching for himself and God. Hasidic message noted as well: "Perhaps we are being taught that crying is not enough,

we must learn to sing."

B268 Capouya, Emil. "The Cry of the Forsaken." Saturday Review, XLIX (May 28, 1966), 32-33.
Mr. Capouya criticizes Wiesel's literary merit. He is cited not as a writer but as a man crying in the wilderness. "He is no artist, but the accuser of an absent God."

B269 Cargas, Harry. "Elie Wiesel as Prophet of the Past." St. Louis Globe-Democrat, May 14, 1966, p. 6-D.
In his discussion of the Chosen People concept, Mr. Cargas cites Wiesel's statement: "The Messiah isn't one man ... he's all men." In his appraisal of the author he states: "Few writers need to be read totally. Wiesel is one. It is almost as if our own salvation were bound up in his."

B270 Cohen, Lustig Elaine. "Der Anklager." Aufbau (New York), August 5, 1966, p. 14.
Review of Gates of the Forest in German.

B271 Corodimas, Peter. Best Sellers, XXVI (June 15, 1966), 126.
G.O.T.F. is called a superb reading experience.

B272 Cromie, Robert. "The Ability to Cast a Spell." Chicago Tribune, May 1, 1966, Sec. 9, p. 4.
Much explication of novel. Biographical comments contain inaccurate information--"Wiesel speaks only French and English." The relationship between Wiesel and Mauriac is noted, and quotes by Rabbi Heschel and S. N. Behrman on Wiesel are given.

B273 Dance, Jim. "When the World Crushed a Boy and He Survived." Detroit Free Press, June 5, 1966, p. 5-B.
Time and reality are explored in this critique. Wiesel is able to capture and sustain a "mood of hallucination in reality."

B274 Davis, Gilbert R. "Nazi Holocaust Given Qualities of Legend." Grand Rapids (Mich.) Press, July 24, 1966, p. 45.
"The novel's ultimate power lies not in its re-creation of the holocaust, but in its larger mythical design."

B275 "Deeply Probing Novel." Sioux City (Iowa) Journal, June 26, 1966, Sec. C, p. 10.
Wiesel's uniqueness, it is felt, stems from his having experienced death, while other writers have only experienced life.

B276 Earl, Ilse. Miami News, July 17, 1966, Miami Magazine Sec., p. 29.
A complete summary type review.

B277 Edelman, Lily. "An Award Winner's Latest." National Jewish Monthly, LXXX (May 1966), 56.
Wiesel's career is reviewed along with information about the holocaust. Mrs. Edelman states that G.O.T.F., along with the earlier books, enable the reader "to walk through the 'gates of the forest' into what Elie Wiesel, drawing upon the kabbalist teachings of his youth, calls 'the orchard of mystic truth.'"

B278 Elman, Richard M. "Betrayed Into Living." New York Times Book Review, June 12, 1966, p. 5.
The review explores the theme of the martyrdom of the survivor who is condemned to live. "His existence is a betrayal of the innocents who perished." Mr. Elman also discusses "who is Jesus and who is Judas." He says that for a moment Wiesel forces us to see that the martyrdom of Christ was the martyrdom of the Jews, recapitulated throughout the generations. "Contains some of Wiesel's most impressive writing since Night."

B279 "False Names." Newsweek, CLXVII (June 13, 1966), 122.
This review discusses the theme of the divorce between a man and his name. The reviewer comments on the question of persecution left unanswered. "The tragedy of incomprehension continues--Wiesel has no better answer for the pogroms then his compatriots in suffering."

B280 Fanning, Garth. Sacramento Bee, July 10, 1966, p. 25.
A descriptive review--mainly positive.

B281 Flanigan, Marion. Providence Journal, June 12, 1966, Sec. W, p. 24.
"Among current adventure novelists, Wiesel stands

like Hyperion in a herd of satyrs. His astonishing intellectual range attests to a life-time of study. Offering a cabbalistic interpretation of the anguish of the Jews he evokes ultimate controversies, which may throw sensitive souls into a state of nightmarish ferment. Those who read him will not forget their prayers."

B282 Fleisher, Leonore. "Paperbacks." Publishers Weekly, CXCI (May 1, 1967), 57.
"If you are not up to the theme of a Godless universe--don't tackle this book."

B283 "Fourth Wiesel Novel Based on Auschwitz." Los Angeles Times, July 24, 1966, Calendar Section, p. 26.
In this analysis, it is felt that the parable about the Baal Shem going into the forest to meditate has little meaning until the end of the book, because "the reader and the hero must first be exposed to a few ideas about the danger in solitude, and the value of human encounters."

B284 Fremont-Smith, Eliot. "The Song and the Dagger." New York Times, May 23, 1966, p. 39.
The protagonist Gregor's search is similar, the reviewer feels, to the author's. It is the theme of "how to be witness." In this book, the reviewer claims, "all men are witnesses, all men are Jews." He continues, "it is the condition of our lives and the song and dagger of Elie Wiesel's art." Reprinted: "Auschwitz Sets Theme of Jewish Survivor's Novel." Hartford Times, May 28, 1966, p. 22, (abridged review) Huntington (W. Va.) Herald Advertiser, May 29, 1966, Amusement Sec., p. 5.

B285 Frisch, D. R. "On the Book Shelf." Minneapolis American Jewish World, January 13, 1967, p. 15.
A mainly descriptive account.

B286 Galloway, David D. "The Highsmith Jewel." The Spectator, No. 7234 (February 17, 1967), p. 201.
A brief review in a list of other reviews. A comparison to Camus is made, and the book is called a "struggle against the daemons of nihilism and despair."

B287 Gardner, John. "More Smog from the Dark Satanic

Mills." Southern Review, V (Winter 1969), 241-242.
"G.O.T.F. though not a great book, has power."

B288 Gatz, Joan. "Allegorical Novel of Jewish Persecution." Omaha World-Herald, August 7, 1966, Magazine Section, p. 31.
The book is considered not wholly successful because of the "elliptical style" which circles the story in an "oblique way." Even though the method of turning horrific events into a form of fable is most effective at times, this reviewer feels that the effect is "at the cost of dramatic fire.... When content is so stressed, action loses out." Nevertheless she concludes by saying: "even though this novel is vaguely unsatisfying, it is also a haunting and compelling story of man and a situation beyond hope."

B289 Gold, Irwin. "Significant Religious Allegory." Los Angeles Times, June 19, 1966, Calendar Sec., p. 28.
"A master novelist, his dramatic scenes are unforgettable." The scene especially singled out for comment--Gregor in deaf-mute disguise reviled in his unwilling role as Judas in the village Passion Play.

B290 Goldstein, David. "From Earth to Heaven." London Jewish Chronicle, March 3, 1967, p. 20.
A review of the British edition. "The book is beautifully translated and should be read slowly, again and again." A reference is made to Wiesel's statement: "God made man because he loves stories." Mr. Goldstein feels that we may add that "man loves God by making stories like this."

B291 Goolrick, Esten. "A World in Which God Made Man to Kill Him." Roanoke (Va.) Times, June 26, 1966, Sec. C, p. 8.
A brief explication of the novel.

B292 Griffin, Dorothea. "Man's Despair Theme of Difficult Novel." Nashville Banner, July 29, 1966, p. 25.
In commenting on the different levels of the book, the critic states: "Between episodes that are, or could be actual, there are interspersed dreams and

visions and nightmares and many stories, all of which are woven into the total theme of man's despair, which is universal, and man's hope which is evanescent and frail."

B293 Handlin, Oscar. "Accepting Life." Atlantic Monthly, CCXVII (June 1966), 135-136.
Mr. Handlin notes that the concern with evil is what is at the heart of this moving novel. Gregor's search for knowledge of himself lead him to accept life as it is.

B294 Hyams, Barry. "Buchenwald Survivors: Novel Traces Victory Over Despair." Philadelphia Inquirer, July 3, 1966, Today's World Sec., p. 7.
Much detail is spent describing Gregor. G.O.T.F. is called "a message from Hell brought by one who has returned from there. Wiesel speaks with a voice that may not be ignored, else the road for us all leads back to the pit."

B295 Kahn, Lothar. "The Jewish Novel." Catholic World, CCIV (January 1967), 242-244.
"Perhaps more than any other Jewish writer today, Elie Wiesel embodies the whole of Jewish life and tradition, with religion for once the paramount interest."

B296 Kirkus, XXXIV (March 15, 1966), 326-327.
Gregor's search for himself leads him to Gavriel, who, in this review, is referred to as a "surrogate Messiah." To need the Messiah, Gregor learns "is in effect to relinquish the faith that he is everywhere: in the defiant laugh of Gavriel, in the son of the Hasidim, and in Auschwitz, too."

B297 Kitching, Jessie. Publishers Weekly, CLXXXIX (April 11, 1966), 55-56.
"A novel of the first rank. The writing is brilliant, evocative, and full of the imagery necessary to sustain the allegorical movement of the novel."

B298 Lawson, David R. "A Kaddish for Victims of Concentration Camps." Savannah News, June 19, 1966, Magazine Sec., p. 9.
Wiesel is compared to Schwartz-Bart in this review. G.O.T.F. is said to deal with two haunting

issues: "How can man believe in a rational God in the light of the Nazi destruction of His people, and what shall a man do when faced with the choice of dying in his faith or living without it." The book is called "worthy and profound." Mention is also made of the B'nai B'rith Jewish Heritage Award.

B299 Lever, Walter. "Ghosts of Auschwitz." London World Jewry, X (May/June, 1967), 27.
"G.O.T.F. attempts to find the way back to a rehabilitation of the human spirit, a re-acceptance of man by God, and of God by man."

B300 Levine, Rose. "Survivor of Auschwitz Writes Moving Novel." Boston Traveler, June 23, 1966, p. 13.
A positive descriptive account.

B301 Levitas, Gloria. "Buchenwald." Chicago Sunday Tribune Book World, October 29, 1967, p. 16.
This review deals with the theme of how man lives with the knowledge of his imminent death. The theme can be probed well, because Wiesel's perspective is inward. The author is at his best, the reviewer feels "when immersed wholly in his religious argument with a God who abandoned him, he recreates the tribal emotions."

B302 Levy, Henry W. "A Paean of Faith." Baltimore Sun, June 12, 1966, Sec. D, p. 5.
After Wiesel wrestles with his conscience, his inner soul and his troubled love, he comes up with, according to this critic, the following conclusions: that "life is worth living, that you can't escape into solitude, that darkness is man's lot as well as light." He calls the book "a paean of faith."

B303 Lynch, Donna. Baton Rouge Advocate, July 24, 1966, Sec. E, p. 2.
A short summary type review.

B304 McCafferty, Laura. "Gates of the Forest Real Piece of Art." Fort Wayne News-Sentinel, September 3, 1966, p. 4-A.
The theme of maniacal laughter is focused on. The novel is termed "a wonderfully constructed piece of art. It has an inner force which gives it depth and poignancy. It tackles the problem which Gregor faces:

How to live in a world that God has abandoned?"

B305 MacNamara, Desmond. New Statesman, LXXII (February 17, 1967), 232.
The reviewer asks "what remains of a Jew who resists and freakishly emerges from the gas ovens?" He says that Wiesel pursues this inquiry in G.O.T.F. and he adds "it is hard at times for a goy to follow him." He goes on to say that "the thickets of Hassidic symbolism are very dense, though they bloom exotically."

B306 "Messiah Than Thou." London Times Literary Supplement, March 2, 1967, p. 161.
The reviewer finds that the allegory of Gregor, the symbolic Jew, "develops at times a certain power and compulsiveness, but on the whole, the book is too turgid."
"Mr. Wiesel's prose booms like a bittern."

B307 Miller, Alicia Metcalf. "Does Time Heal All Wounds?" Cleveland Plain Dealer, June 26, 1966, p. 8-F.
Wiesel's story-telling ability is lauded. G.O.T.F. is called a "highly complex book, yet written with the simplicity and beauty of a folk-tale." Wiesel is said to speak, in the deepest sense, to the twentieth century conscience.

B308 "Narrative Challenges Intellect." Allentown (Pa.) Call Chronicle, June 19, 1966, Sec. E, p. 5.
A positive descriptive review.

B309 New Yorker, XLII (August 20, 1966), 133.
In a brief review, the reviewer comments on Wiesel's deportation to Auschwitz as a child, and feels that the confusion with the world that Wiesel felt is expressed in this "remarkably affecting story."

B310 Perley, Maie E. "Suspense Novel Details Man's Spiritual Growth." Louisville Times, May 26, 1966, Sec. A, p. 11.
Much delineation of the character of Gregor, the protagonist. "It is a superbly balanced work that plays humor against tragedy. Its appeal is to the many who are concerned with the spiritual drift of our times."

B311 Poller, Marion. Library Journal, XCI (May 15, 1966), 2525.

In a largely descriptive review, the following comment is noted: "Elie Wiesel is telling not only an excellent story, but also a four part parable about God's and man's inhumanity to man." It is listed as highly recommended.

B312 Reid, Walter, Glasgow Herald, February 18, 1967, p. 9.

The "defiant heroism" that surges throughout the book is noted. It is called "an irritating book to read, often wooly and gravid with allegory, but a rewarding one." "Though it is richly embellished with Jewish folk tales and tradition; its application is universal, its significance extends to all who ask with Gregor, 'After what has happened to us, how can you believe in God?'"

B313 *Riemer, Rabbi Jack. Dayton Jewish Chronicle, May 12, 1966.

After a sketch of the book, Rabbi Riemer says that Wiesel's books must be read in their totality to be appreciated. "They are in my judgment not novels, but seforim, holy books, the diary of a tortured and a holy soul."

B314 Rogoff, Hillel. "Eliezar Vizel S'Niaar Roman: De Tviaran fun Veld." New York Daily Forward, June 5, 1966, Sec. 2, p. 5.

Yiddish review.

B315 Rogozini, Norman. "Reality in a Myth to Describe Horror." Cleveland Press, August 26, 1966, Showcase Sec., p. 17.

This critique shows how Wiesel's account of the Holocaust differs from others who deal in names, dates and statistics; "... by weaving myth, Elie Wiesel succeeds in exploring the emotional experience of the millions who were hunted."

B316 Rothermel, J. T. "He Poses Mystery in Deepest Sense." Birmingham (Ala.) News, May 29, 1966, Sec. E, p. 7.

Wiesel's use of allegory, myth, and the idea of a God who permits suffering are explored here.

B317 Schott, Webster. "Anger at a God That Failed." Life, LX (June 10, 1966), 17.
Mr. Schott calls G.O.T.F. a metaphor for the escape from blackness and a search for light. He feels that Gregor cannot convincingly renovate a God that has failed. "Hope sprung eternal from such ashes is beyond Wiesel's literary capacities."

B318 Sharp, Jay H. "Harvest of Jewish Themes." Kansas City (Mo.) Star, December 25, 1966, Sec. E, p. 5.
Appears in a review along with other book on Jewish themes. Calls G.O.T.F. "profoundly moving--brilliant." Theme of making peace with a God who has abandoned the hero is focused on.

B319 Slomovitz, Phil. "Elie Wiesel's Prize-Winning The Gates of the Forest Gains New Status for Famous Author." Detroit Jewish News, May 20, 1966, p. 16.
Mr. Slomovitz points to the book's significance as not only a great contribution to the literature of the holocaust, but as a work that is described as "immense" because of its vivid description and poetic style as well. In using an example of Hasidic folklore from the novel, he states: "it is in this spirit that a great drama is unfolded--poetically narrated, incorporating action, heart-rending description of the Nazi terror mingled with human reactions that contain humor as well as pathos."

B320 Smith, Miles. "Novel Full of Symbols, Allegory." Oakland (Cal.) Tribune, June 6, 1966, p. 23.
Associated Press descriptive account.

B321 Spear, Sheri. Cheyenne (Wyo.) State-Tribune, October 29, 1966, p. 10.
Contains much summary. The autobiographical nature of the book is noted, and the reviewer adds: "it is the author's experience with man's inhumanity to man that is the basis of the power and feeling which dominate Gates of the Forest.

B322 Spencer, Robin C. "Concentration Inmate Tells of Horrors." New Britain (Conn.) Herald, July 5, 1966, p. 12.
An explication with positive critical comment.

B323 St. Goar, Maria. "The Gates of the Forest." Chattanooga (Tenn.) Times, September 18, 1966, p. 20. "The reader is frequently lost in this dark forest of allegory, fantasy and imagination, he finally sees daylight in the last illuminating chapters of the book."

B324 Sullivan, Irene. "Recounting Mental Pains of Jews Under Hitler." Lexington (Ky.) Herald-Leader, June 12, 1966, p. 64.
A short explanatory review.

B325 *"Symbols of Life." High Point (N.C.) Enterprise, May 29, 1966.
A summary type review.

B326 Thompson, Francis J. "Another Settlement." Tampa Tribune, August 21, 1966, Accent Sec., p. 32.
Concentrates on Christ killing epithets used in the book, referred to as "German scurrilities." He then makes reference to the [then] current world situation: "But how can we be shocked by this when we ignore the same out of contemporary St. Petersburg (Leningrad)?"

B327 Wain, John. "The Insulted and Injured." New York Review of Books, VII (July 28, 1966), 22-23.
Review is concerned with the themes of identity and Judas. "G.O.T.F. is one of those books like Dr. Zhivago; that restores one's faith in life by wrestling with a despair too huge to be described." Reviewed along with The Last Gentleman by Walker Percy and The Night Visitor and Other Stories by B. Traven.

B328 Walsh, Anne C. "Novelist Tells of Search for God." Phoenix (Ariz.) Gazette, July 13, 1966, p. 68.
Search themes explored.

B329 Wardle, Irving. London Observer, February 19, 1967, Observer Review Section, p. 26.
The novel is described as a "deeply Jewish work which reflects a monstrous experience in terms of allegory and folk-lore." The critic feels that it would be impertinent for anyone but another survivor to "review" a book like this. "But the passionately compressed writing (the eloquent translation by Frances Frenaye) makes one trust everything that Wiesel has to say."

B330 Weinberg, Helen. "Elie Wiesel's Redemptive Quest." Congress Bi-Weekly, XXXIII (November 7, 1966), 27-29.

In a detailed review, the following themes are covered: (1) Judas theme; (2) the division of the book into seasons; (3) Kaddish theme. In conclusion the reviewer states: "By his art, Wiesel has restructured history so as to return meaningful names to the millions who died, nameless, as numbers."

B331 White, Victor. "Presence of Death, Menace of Life." Dallas News, June 19, 1966, Sec. F, p. 8.

The reviewer, a faculty member at a Dallas Catholic school, takes notice of the challenging of God, which is so central to the novel. "It is strong fare, perhaps the sort of fare to be expected in an age that flirts with the concept that 'God is Dead.' Elie Wiesel's achievement is that so much in this frequently terrifying record of one man's search for identity is shot through with a fierce, eerie beauty, that his characters have a haunting vitality, and that the story is told by a master craftsman."

B332 Whitman, Digby B. "A Man Condemned to Life." Chicago Sunday Tribune Books Today, May 22, 1966, p. 13.

The reviewer says as in Dawn, Wiesel deals with the same intolerable paradox of freedom without choice. "Man is not permitted but compelled to work out his own destiny and to do so independently of his creator."

B333 Wilkins, Mary Vann. "Searching for the Answers." Greensboro (N.C.) News, July 3, 1966, Sec. D, p. 3.

The work is called "an allegory, a catechism." Even though the questions are worth asking, this reviewer feels that G.O.T.F. "degenerates into Mr. Wiesel's own rather personal wandering search."

B334 Winegarten, Renee. "Elie Wiesel: Disquieting Messenger." Jewish Observer and Mid-East Review (London), XVI (March 17, 1967), 17.

A well-written positive review. The reviewer says of the author, "He has found that the only way to encompass the unspeakable experiences of his youth is not through the unadorned recital of fact favored by some, but through the cryptic poetry of Hasidic allegory, familiar to him from childhood." His use of French logical thought in addition to Hasidic logic of spirit combine, according to this account, to force a combination of cabalistic mysticism with the questing dialectic of contemporary French humanism."

B335 Woods, Harriet. "A Challenge to Faith." St. Louis Post-Dispatch, June 26, 1966, Sec. C, p. 4.
The book is termed "a magnificent blend of myth and realism." Wiesel is said to have succeeded in turning the horror of the Nazi final solution into "a timeless challenge to man's faith and spirit."

B336 Zachary, Hugh. "Novel on Nazi Horror." Raleigh (N.C.) Observer, July 3, 1966, sec. 3, p. 3.
"To a reader not familiar with Jewish mythology, the story seems to skirt the very real horror of the murder of millions, and loses itself in vague mysticism."

THE JEWS OF SILENCE

B337 *Bean, George. "Russian Jewry." London Jewish Gazette, May 16, 1969.
In speaking of the silence of the Jews outside the Soviet Union, this reviewer says of Wiesel, "His accusation is at once a rebuke and a challange."

B338 Booklist, LXIII (March 15, 1967), 747.
A brief descriptive review.

B339 Brumberg, Abraham. "Despite the Thaw." The Reporter, XXXVI (March 9, 1967), 60-62.
An historical background to the Jews in Russia is given. The reviewer feels that Wiesel has been able to convey the most essential truth about the Soviet Union, "that irrespective of the parallels to other suspect groups; the Jews are subjected to maltreatment and repression because they are Jews and as Jews."

B340 Cang, Joel. "Inside the U.S.S.R." World Jewry (London), XII (January/February 1969), 18-19.
Mention is made of the "eyes" of the Jews that followed Wiesel throughout Russia. "A stirring, highly emotional picture of the situation in Russia."

B341 Cargas, Harry J. "A Reporter's Look at Soviet Jewry." Edmonston (Canada) Western Catholic Reporter, January 19, 1967.

Much material by and about Wiesel is cited. Of The Jews of Silence: "His efforts are not made in hating Russians but in loving Jews."

Mr. Cargas, who has since nominated Wiesel for the Nobel Prize delivers a poignant encomium to the author: "The man that I think is the finest living writer is unknown to most of the world."

B342 Grusd, Edward E. "Soviet Jewry: A Paradox." National Jewish Monthly, LXXI (February 1967), 32-33.

The "paradox" is the simultaneous grievous and hopeful nature of the condition of the Soviet Jews as presented by Wiesel.

B343 Handlin, Oscar. The Atlantic, CCXVII (December 1966), 147.

"There is a silence beyond the Iron Curtain, but we ought not to mistake it for consent."

B344 Hayward, Max. Commentary, XLIII (March 1967), 91-92.

The historical material on conditions of Soviet Jewry is presented by reviewer. He says that Wiesel's book reminds us that "the fate of Russian Jewry still vitally depends on being held constantly in the public eye abroad."

B345 Joravsky, David. "The Absurdity of the Jewish Condition." The Nation, CCIV (May 22, 1967), 661.

The reviewer says that "Wiesel breathes holy fire." He cites Wiesel's conclusion that only Soviet Jews hold on to the true faith, because only they are isolated and oppressed.

B346 Kahn, Lothar. American Zionist, LVII (January 1967), 25.

The reviewer says that silence has been a high frequency word in the novels of Elie Wiesel. It is also the language of the dead (Auschwitz) and it is also the language of the witness. He notes, as do most reviews of this book, Wiesel's concern with the eyes of Soviet Jews. He feels that even though The Jews of Silence is flawed by rhetoric and seeming contradictions at times, it's must reading.

B347 Kirkus, XXXIV (September 1, 1966), 960.
A brief, positive, mainly descriptive review.

B348 Kitching, Jessie. Publishers Weekly, CXC (October 17, 1966), 60-61.
The reviewer calls the book a moving one, singling out for comment the chapter about the massacre ground of Babi Yar in Kiev.

B349 Kupferberg, Herbert. "A Sense of Separateness." Book Week, May 7, 1967, p. 13.
Mr. Kupferberg mentions the distinction Wiesel makes between the plight of Jews in the Soviet Union and those of Nazi Germany: "The difference, he [Wiesel] notes simply, is that between life and death." Nevertheless, the Soviet Union plight is told fully. It is called a "beautifully written book," one in which the theme of hope is present.

B350 Laqueur, Walter. "People Without a Country." New York Review of Books, VIII (March 23, 1967), 22-24.
"This is a powerful and moving little book, very well translated from the Hebrew. It is based on mystic belief, and one hesitates to discuss it in rational terms."

B351 Leviant, Curt. "Behind the Hills of Darkness." Congress Bi-Weekly, XXXIV (February 6, 1967), 18.
Wiesel's indictment is double-edged the reviewer asserts. "It faces the Soviet regime with its deeds, and Western Jews with their silence."

B352 Luther, Catherine. "Apathy Appalling." Albuquerque (N.M.) Journal, March 13, 1967, Sec. A, p. 5.
"Reading The Jews of Silence one is presented with an awesome picture of what we thought had ended with W.W. II. The camps and gas chambers apparently ended, but the persecution has not."

B353 Newman, William. Library Journal, XCI (December 1, 1966), 5964.
The reviewer cites the work, not for its reportage, but for "the moral indignation and anguish that are ex-

pressed in this melancholy book." It is highly recommended.

B354 New Yorker, XLII (February 18, 1967), 168.
"Although the book deals with actual people and actual situations that the author encountered on a trip to Russia, it is not journalistic, but subjective and poetic."

B355 The Observer (London), March 30, 1969, Observer Review Sec., p. 29.
Wiesel does not appear as a propagandist, according to this critic. "He merely wished to record what it means to be a Jew in Russia today, to establish a memorial for the living, and he does so movingly."

B356 "Paperback Fiction." Publishers Weekly, CXCII (October 23, 1967), 54.
A review of the Signet paperback version of Jews of Silence. Calls it an emotional book, and speaks of the surging and unshakeable faith of Russian Jewry.

B357 Pryce-Jones, David. "Russian Jews Keep Faith." London Telegraph, January 26, 1969, p. 13.
Wiesel's feelings and experiences are interpreted as follows: "The Jews of Silence throbs with the pain and the hope which he [Wiesel] feels will grow out of that pain. He gropes for insight into what it means to believe in God, to be a Jew, to overcome enemies and yet remain humane. As he gropes, he ceases to be a novelist and a visitor to Russia. His report becomes something devotional, a bearing of witness, a prayer."

B358 Rubin, Ronald I. "Russia and the Scattered Ones." Christian Science Monitor, December 30, 1966, Sec. II, p. 9.
"Wiesel does not portray a self-pitying Soviet Jewry. Rather he stresses the indomitable strength of their belief."

B359 Ruskin, Pamela. Australian Jewish News (Melbourne), XXXV (April 3, 1969), 9.
Wiesel's message of the need to cry out is stressed. Much note is made of the sensitivity of the presentation.

B360 Salisbury, Harrison E. Hadassah Magazine, XLVIII (December 1966), 16-17.
Concentrates in his review on Wiesel's pinpointing the Russian Jewry problem. "There is the central question--the question of fear."

B361 Saper, Arthur Saul. "Grim Tenacity of Soviet Jewry." Zionist Record and South African Jewish Chronicle (Johannesburg), March 14, 1969, p. 15.
A lengthy in-depth review.

B362 Schwartz, Harry. "Survival of the Soviet Synagogue." Saturday Review, XLIX (November 26, 1966), 42.
The reviewer, a Russian scholar, compares his views of a visit to Russia with those of Wiesel's. He feels that Wiesel ends with more hope.

B363 Singer, Isaac Bashevis. New York Times Book Review, January 8, 1967, Sec. 7, p. 16.
Mr. Singer calls The Jews of Silence "one passionate outcry, both in content and in style." He sums up Wiesel's message from Soviet Jews to World Jewry quoting from the book: "Cry out, cry out, until you have no more strength to cry."

B364 Siskin, Edgar E. "An Affirmation of Identity." Chicago Sunday Tribune Books Today, January 1, 1967, p. 5.
"Elie Wiesel is coming to be recognized as the authentic chronicler of the Jewish tragedy of our time."

B365 Stern, Daniel. Commonweal, LXXXVI (May 12, 1967), 232-234.
This review reinforces the idea expressed in many of the reviews of this book, that Wiesel gives no answers concerning the Jewishness of Russian Jews, he gives the questions.

B366 Tessler, Gloria. "Redemption in Russia." Jewish Observer and Middle East Review (London), XVIII (March 7, 1969), 21.
Wiesel is spoken of as an impressionist. "His writing is naked and devoid of adjective," but this is made up for the reviewer feels, in Wiesel's mastery of mood and emotion.

B367 Wohlgelernter, Maurice. "Out of the Depths." Tradition, IX (Spring-Summer 1967), 169-175.
The review compares Jews of Silence with other documentary accounts of Jewish life in Russia. There is also an account of Wiesel's second trip to Russia in October of 1966. The reviewer concludes with Wiesel's findings, that destiny needs to be taken into the hands of the Soviet Jews themselves, because as they (the Russian Jews) sadly realize, help is not forthcoming.

B368 Ziman, H. D. "Weizmann as a Zionist Junior." London Daily Telegraph, February 6, 1969, p. 22.
In a review that appears with others on Jewish subjects, Wiesel is called "very wordy and sentimental: for any facts one has to turn to the historical afterword by his translator, Neal Kosodoy."

THE TOWN BEYOND THE WALL (reissued 1967)

B369 Ancrum, Calhoun. "Elie Wiesel's Book Proves His Worth." Charleston (S.C.) News and Courier, October 22, 1967, p. 3-D.
The reissuing of T.B.T.W. is an important event because "it is becoming increasingly evident that Mr. Wiesel is a contemporary prophet and one of the truly significant living writers. His symbolism and metaphor are rich and poetic; his writing is informed with vigorous Hasidic mysticism. To read him is an adventure of mind and spirit, leaving one forever altered and enriched.... How the narrator finds consolation and redemption under new suffering is part of the magic of Elie Wiesel's great art as a writer and thinker. It is exciting to see in one's own time the arrival of great works."

B370 Edelman, Lily. "Is Anybody Listening?" National Jewish Monthly, LXXXIV (June 1970), 44 (A review of the Bard/Avon edition).
Mrs. Edelman, in an essay-review on the "dialogue of the deaf," cites Michael, the hero-narrator of T.B.T.W., "trapped in a prison cell behind the Iron Curtain, who keeps trying to communicate with his only companion a deaf-mute. Michael concludes with 'the essence of man is to be question, and the es-

sence of the question is to be without answer.'"

B371 Miller, Alicia Metcalf. "Bitter Jew Finds Revenge in Contempt." Cleveland Plain Dealer, October 15, 1967, p. H-8.

In commenting on the reissuing, this critic thinks that T.B.T.W. does not have the power of the other novels--possibly, she feels, because it is not as personal as the others. "It lacks the spontaneity and the striking mythical quality that mark his other works.... Characterizations are wooden and underdeveloped, and in spots Wiesel's usually flawless prose is far too deliberate and studied."

B372 Perley, Maie E. "Story of a Jew's Return to Hungary is a Profound Spiritual Experience." Louisville Times, January 11, 1968, p. A-13.

The reviewer traces Michael's, the protagonist, physical as well as spiritual journey. His adventures are "interwoven with finely wrought legends." To do justice to this work in a review is likened to laying hands on a dream. "Suffice it to say that the book is a profound spiritual experience."

B373 Polk, Peggy. "Prize Novel is Re-Issued." Augusta (Ga.) Chronicle-Herald, November 5, 1967, p. 15D.

Wiesel is referred to as an author who writes with a Biblical simplicity and dignity. "Though the book is a tragic tale it is full of wry humor and memorable characters." The town drunk and slut are singled out especially. Reprinted: Tulsa (Okla.) World, January 21, 1968, p. 14.

B374 Siggins, Clara M. Best Sellers, XXVII (November 1, 1967), 309-310.

Talks about reissuing as coming at the right moment. "The story forces us to realize that we are not freed of responsibility for the present and the future." The reviewer compares the theme of T.B.T.W. with the theme of Hochhuth's "The Deputy." "Man's greatest sin is his apathy towards evil."

B375 Sneider, Vern. "A Survivor of a Nazi Camp and Why He Went Home." Detroit Free Press, October 29, 1967, p. 5-B.

Concerning the re-issuing: "It should be included in any listing of the best novels of the year." He speaks of all the "returns" made by the hero, Michael. "This is a novel of the mind, the feelings, and the heart. As such it is one of the best to come along in many a moon."

B376 "Sojourner in a Land Haunted by the Spectre of Indifference." Fayetteville Observer (N.C.), October 29, 1967, p. 3-F.
Good summary with little critical comment.

B377 Stone, Leonard W. Hartford Courant, October 15, 1967, Magazine Sec., p. 15.
A favorable review in which comments on the theme of those who did nothing during the holocaust is featured.

B378 Subotnik, Norman. "Wiesel Examines Man's Nature." Baltimore Sun, November 19, 1967, Sec. D, p. 5.
The re-issuing of T.B.T.W. is said to have come at a timely point in history. It is reviewed in retrospect to the Israeli Six Day War.

B379 Zagoren, Ruby. "Elie Wiesel's Prize Novel Republished." Hartford Times, November 10, 1968, p. 9-G.
"This book is not for those who prefer happy endings. It is rather for the reader who sees the universality of man's dreams, even in suffering."

LEGENDS OF OUR TIME

B380 Adams, Phoebe. The Atlantic, CCXXII (November 1968), 144.
A brief descriptive review.

B381 Alter, Robert. "Probing Pain for a Definition of Man." Saturday Review, LI (October 19, 1968), 31.
Mr. Alter says that Wiesel differs from other Holocaust writers in that he [Wiesel] tries to locate a moral perspective from which to view the Holocaust. "L.O.O.T. is written with a blurring of fact and fiction--giving the book a spiritual strength."

B382 Ascherson, Neal. "Survivors." New York Review of Books, XI (January 2, 1969), 28.
The review details the stories. It singles out for special note "The Wandering Jew," "Appointment with

Hate," "An Old Acquaintance." Mr. Ascherson calls the volume "writing of the highest quality." He goes on to say, "It is also history; the final light of art upon that unbearable controversy about those who went unresisting to their death."

B383 Bandler, Michael J. "Why Auschwitz? The Answer: Silence." Christian Science Monitor, November 21, 1968, p. 9.

Elie Wiesel is called "the literary laureate of the Holocaust, the sweetest singer of the most bitter and tragic era of our times." The reviewer deals with the theme of the world during the Holocaust and during the twenty-five years since. He also concerns himself with the material on Eichmann in the book. These areas have been tackled by Wiesel with such force and stylistic drive the reviewer continues, "that leaves the reader stunned, and should lead to a rethinking of each person's private involvement."

B384 Batshaw, Harry Justice. "Spokesman for the Vanished Six Millions." Montreal Star, April 12, 1969, Entertainment sec., p. 6.

Individual comments on most of the tales which are called "a collection of brilliant essays and stories in which [Wiesel] invokes the memories of the dead and living in his life."

B385 Booklist, LXV (December 15, 1968), 434.

The collection is termed "a poetic and sometimes eerie medley of memoir and portrayal of prophetic characters." It goes on to say that the "brooding quality of style raises to a new intensity the realization of an incomparable tragedy."

B386 Bortniker, R. Elijah. Jewish Education, XXXIX (July 1969), 45-46.

An individual review of the stories. "The Last Return" is singled out as the most powerful piece in the collection.

B387 Chaplin, George. Honolulu Star-Bulletin and Advertiser, September 29, 1968, Aloha sec., p. 26.

A short positive explication.

B388 Christian Century, LXXV (October 16, 1968), 1306.

A thumbnail sketch.

B389 Cohen, Martin A. Library Journal, XCIII (September 15, 1968), 3142.
A summary review. It says that the fifteen stories in the book explore the meaning and purpose of life.

B390 Daughtrey, Anita. "Literary Power: Elie Wiesel's Tales." Fresno (Cal.) Bee, October 20, 1968, sec. F, p. 39.
The tales are each unique, but each piece has in common with the others "the benefit of Wiesel's extraordinary awareness and literary power."

B391 Edelman, Lily. B'nai B'rith Woman's World, LIX (December 1968), 6.
"The subdued fire and fury of his [Wiesel's] self-imposed imperative to keep telling the Jewish story stoke his newest work in English, Legends of Our Time, a series of tableaux on Jewish life in our time: their luminous intensity scorches the mind."

B392 Finn, James. "Understanding Auschwitz." New Republic, CLIX (December 14, 1968), 35-36.
The reviewer tries to assimilate the material from a variety of viewpoints, and states: "We will as Christians, Jews and unbelievers, assimilate in time the Holocaust as best we can."

B393 Gilbert, Arthur. The Reconstructionist, XXXII (February 5, 1971), 25. (Review of Bard/Avon edition).
"Elie Wiesel is the most exciting literary theologian of our generation."

B394 Goldberg, Emanuel. "Did Auschwitz Kill the World's Heart?" Boston Herald, December 1, 1968, Christmas Book sec., p. 2.
"The scope and penetration of the work are mesmeric, even superb, especially where contrived legend surmounts fact in authenticity."

B395 Goldberg, Harold. "Legends of Our Time." Intermountain Jewish News (Denver), March 21, 1969, p. 8.
"A Plea for the Dead" is given special notice.

B396 Goldstein, Lawrence. "Memory and Revelation."

The Nation, CCVII (February 24, 1969), 250.
An analytical review of each of the legends. "L.O.O.T. is a celebration of the liberation of memory from horror too terrible to be recounted or dismissed."

B397 Greenfield, Jerome. Jewish Frontier, XXXVI (September 1969), 32-39.
An in-depth review of individual stories. The reviewer feels that Wiesel succeeds in making us a bit more cognizant of our guilt and impotence. "This is a book that few others can match in its moral seriousness and in its sense of metaphysical pain."

B398 Halberstam, Rita. "A Legend of Our Time." New York Jewish Press, January 3, 1969, p. 17.
Elie Wiesel is called a "legend of our time." The stories in this collection are called "tormenting, they ask questions, they give the soul no peace, only pain and torment."

B399 Hall, Joan J. "Why Did They Go?" Houston Post, October 20, 1968, Spotlight Sec., p. 15.
In this analysis, the reviewer chooses to dwell on the question of why did the Jews go to their death.

B400 Hammer, Robert Allan. "The Voice of All Who Died." The Reconstructionist, XXV (May 2, 1969), 26-28.
"When Elie Wiesel writes, the tremor that seizes the world is the echo of the voices of the dead speaking again."
An in-depth review of the individual stories.

B401 Jacobs, Sonia L. "Genocide Reasons Sought." Denver Post, November 3, 1968, Roundup Sec., p. 16.
The central theme of the book as outlined here is "the meaningless death of six million Jews, causing unbelievable despair in this century."

B402 Kern, Robert W. "The Jews in Germany: Before and After." Riverside (Cal.) Enterprise, December 8, 1968, sec. C, p. 3.
L.O.O.T. is reviewed along with Post-Mortem by Leo Katcher. A review of the European Jewish society that the book chronicles is given. The story, "Testament of a Jew from Saragossa," is given criti-

cal comment.

B403 Kipnis, Tina. American Zionist, LIX (December 1968), 30-31.
A brief descriptive review.

B404 Kirkus, XXXVI (August 1, 1968), 880.
"A fierce and moving continuation of the dialogue of those who will not forget."

B405 Margolin, Morton L. "Searing Report of Death Camp." Rocky Mountain News (Denver), November 3, 1968, Startime sec., p. 14.
"The book winds up with an analysis of hate as motivation for revenge and finds it lacking." On Wiesel's ability to communicate the horror: "The flames leap out and sear the reader, too."

B406 Nissenson, Hugh. "A Sequel to the Sacred History of Our Era." New York Times Book Review, January 12, 1969, pp. 34-35.
The reviewer feels that because Elie Wiesel has personally experienced the Holocaust as a religious Jew for whom nothing was profane and everything could be sactified by human endeavor, each encounter therefore, if properly understood, "is a revelation of the sublime." Wiesel's writing, the reviewer continues, has attained the quality of deeds in L.O.O.T. "They are equivalent to Mitzvot, those injunctions of the Torah performed by religious Jews to sanctify the world."

B407 Oregonian (Portland), November 17, 1968, Sec. F, p. 3.
The book is called "enlightening" but not "entertaining." It is a book "of the cruel paradoxes of our time."

B408 Ozick, Cynthia. "The Uses of Legend: Elie Wiesel as Tsaddik." Congress Bi-Weekly, XXXVI (June 9, 1969), 16-20.
A very fine review-essay. Mrs. Ozick says the purpose of legend is to judge. She comments fully on the role of the "rebbe."

B409 Pantell, Hope. "Recalling the Jewish Slaughter." Washington Star, November 13, 1968, Sec. F, p. 11.

Discusses the idea of the dead being abandoned by the living. The reviewer sees Wiesel's mission as one that evokes painful memories and asks agonizing questions. Special note is given to "Appointment With Hate" and "A Plea For the Dead."

B410 Perlingieri, G. John. "'Legends' is Pure Sensitivity." Miami Hurricane, March 26, 1971, p. 8.
"'Legends' gives the reader in one stroke, a glimpse of the inside--the inside of the mind, soul, and a period of history whose entire existence despoils the civilized mind."

B411 Pusey, William W. III. "We've No Right to Judge Them." Roanoke (Va.) Times, February 16, 1969, sec. C, p. 9.
Places the emphasis of the book on the examination of the large questions of guilt and of resistance.

B412 *Rabin, Morry. Long Beach (Cal.) Press-Telegram, January 19, 1969.
Wiesel's portrayal of the Jewish resistance is said to have a strong effect and much dignity.

B413 Richler, Mordecai. "Spokesman for the Dead." New Leader, LI (December 30, 1968), 19-20.
An encomium to Wiesel. "His continuing testimony and unequalled insights into the Holocaust are of incomparable importance to us all."

B414 Riemer, Jack. "A Song of Hope." Boston Jewish Advocate, October 3, 1968, Sec. 2, p. 3.
An essay-review on Wiesel's style and genre. "Elie Wiesel writes neither history nor fiction, but a new kind of prose, a modern form of myth.... The most astonishing thing about all of his writings is the gentleness of his tone and the kindness of his spirit." Reprinted: Hadassah Magazine, L (November 1968), 20.

B415 Rumley, Larry. "The Trauma of Auschwitz." Seattle Times, January 12, 1969, Magazine Sec., p. 18.
Historical background information given about Auschwitz. "To read this, in the compelling prose of Elie Wiesel, is to weep. Not just for the victims who died in the camps, but for all of us."

B416 Scratch, Walter L. Santa Monica (Cal.) Evening Outlook, January 18, 1969, Outlook West Magazine Sec., p. 14.
A brief explanatory review.

B417 Silver, Adele Z. "Painful Reading But a Contagious Fever." Cleveland Plain Dealer, October 20, 1968, Sec. H, p. 8.
This appraisal comments on how painful the reading of this book is, and how much more painful it must be to write. "One who is beset by the horrors of the world is the kind of reader who would look to Wiesel for companionship. He offers no other consolations--but then neither does history."

B418 Slomovitz, Philip. "Wiesel's Legends of Our Time Cries Out for Justice, Reminds Readers of Holocaust." Detroit Jewish News, December 6, 1968, p. 16.
After much individual discussion of the stories, the collection as a whole is termed another "J'accuse." "It is another great work by one of our most brilliant writers."

B419 Sparrow, Prep. "A Failure of 2,000 Years of Christian Civilization." Fayettville (N.C.) Observer, November 3, 1968, Sec. D, p. 3.
He voices truths that few writers of this generation can or are willing to express.

B420 Stern, Daniel. "A Voice To Trust in an Age of Suspicion." Book World, II (October 20, 1968), 9.
Mr. Stern says that the tales invoke overtones of mystery, of folklore, of parable. He singles out "The Last Return," and predicts that it will become a classic. "Wiesel uses the strange and endless destiny of the Jews as victim as a means of exploring good and evil."

B421 Subotnik, Norman. "Possessed by Other's Guilt." Baltimore Sun, October 6, 1968, Sec. D, p. 5.
Mr. Subotnik addresses himself to the theme of indifference that pervades the tales. "Meanwhile Mr. Wiesel and his dybbuk suffer for all who are guilty of the sin of indifference. And whether it be indifference to Auschwitz, Vietnam, Biafra or Watts--who is innocent of that sin?"

B422 Wagner, Nancy. "Jew Issues Indictment of Apathy." Minneapolis Tribune, October 27, 1968, Sec. E, p. 6.

On first glance, this book would not appear to be appropriate for "mod" people, this critic states. Nevertheless, she notes, "These are perhaps the very people to whom the message should be directed, for it brings into sharp focus the terrifying results of complacent apathy." "A Plea for the Dead" is made mention of.

B423 Walker, Robert. "A Brilliant Collection." Houston Chronicle, November 24, 1968, Zest Magazine Sec., p. 14.

"In these stories there is a passionate outcry toward a definition of man."

B424 White, Edward M. "Days of Auschwitz and Before." Los Angeles Times, November 3, 1968, Calendar Sec., p. 34.

"Wiesel's extraordinary achievement has been the creation of coherent art embodying with honesty irreconcilable conflicts."

B425 Wohlgelernter, Maurice. "Legends for All Time." American Zionist, LX (September 1969), 39-41.

An excellent essay review. The reviewer states that the only heightened imaginative force that can match Wiesel's treatment of the Holocaust is the State of Israel. "For that, surely, is the greatest legend of our time."

B426 Wolff, Geoffrey. "Surviving Auschwitz." Washington Post, October 26, Sec. A, p. 16.

Much comparison to Job is made. "Job refused to curse God; Wiesel refuses to remain silent."

B427 Woods, Harriet. "Miseries Remembered." St. Louis Post Dispatch, October 20, 1968, Sec. C, p. 4.

"In these stories the dead not only live again, but hand on a special heritage. Wiesel's own suffering and art turn their simple humanity into legends for all time."

B428 Young, Melvin. "Perspectives." Chattanooga (Tenn.) Times, January 5, 1969, Sec. B, p. 2.

Wiesel's concept of giving no answers is stressed.

B429 Zingman, Barbara. "Reflections On Murder and Hate." Louisville Times, March 3, 1969, Sec. A, p. 9.
"A Plea for the Dead" is featured. Comments on the author's source of myth and legends for universal truths, rather than supposed "true histories."

A BEGGAR IN JERUSALEM

B430 Bandler, Michael J. "I Shout and So I Am." Christian Science Monitor, February 19, 1970, Sec. B, p. 11.
The reviewer scores Wiesel's use of language in his account of the capture of the Old City. He cites much material from the book to substantiate his praise for Wiesel's mastery of language.

B431 ________. "New Jewish Paperbacks." Hadassah Magazine, LII (June 1971), 25. (Review of Avon Paperback)
"Wiesel's account of the Israeli capture of the Old City of Jerusalem is worth the entire price of this meaningful book."

B432 Bannon, Barbara A. Publishers Weekly, CXCVI (November 17, 1969), 79.
"Wiesel too often permits his extensive and authoritative knowledge of Jewish myths, legends, theology to slow the pace of the narrative."

B433 Brady, Charles A. "Two Similar Novels by Jewish Authors Actually Far Apart." Buffalo News, February 21, 1970, Sec. B, p. 8.
(Reviewed together with Mr. Sammler's Planet by Saul Bellow.)
The early sequences of B. in J. are singled out as being "hauntingly moving." They realize Wiesel's ambition of producing a book which will be at once a "psalm, a paean and a prophecy." Nevertheless the reviewer feels that three-quarters through the book "the delicately poised movement breaks down into merely rhetoric."

B434 Brin, Ruth F. "Adventures of a Beggar--a Madman--

in Jerusalem." Minneapolis Tribune, March 1, 1970, Sec. E, p. 14.
The review concerns itself with the universal applicability of Jewish mysticism and also with Wiesel's role as witness.

B435 *Burton, Hal. "Israel in Apocalypse." Newsday, January 24, 1970.
Concentrates on the theme of Jerusalem as the symbol of Jewish survival.

B436 *Callaghan, Barry. "Alive with the Need to Wear God as His Crown." Toronto Telegram, February 14, 1970.
The critic analyzes the definition of the character of Katriel's name, i.e., "God be my crown."

B437 Capitanchik, Maurice. The Spectator, CCXXV (July 25, 1970), 77.
Wiesel's writing is criticized as "portentous and uneven and partly turgid--sometimes almost banal.... But it authentically represents an ancient, traditionalist view, which is also its limitation."

B438 Comp, Samuel R. Best Sellers, XXIX (March 15, 1970), 476-477.
Mr. Comp states that in Wiesel's search for answers to his own questions, he becomes so deeply involved with his own emotional reactions that the picture portrayed, perhaps, falls slightly short of being realistic.

B439 Coppel, Alfred. "Diamonds in a Vein of Clay." San Francisco Examiner, February 8, 1970, "This World" Sec., p. 38.
B. in J. is compared to Andre Schwartz-Bart's, The Last of the Just.
"When Jewish soldiers took the Old City of Jerusalem, a people regained its heart. Wiesel's book makes this crystal clear."

B440 Currie, Teresita. "A Powerful Lyrical Work." Foreign Service Journal, XLVII (May 1970), 44.
The book is called "a tale, a web of tales, its messages the most gripping because they are never made explicit."

B441 Dellinger, Maxwell Anne. "In Search of Understanding." Greensboro (N.C.) News, February 15, 1970, Sec. B, p. 3.
A positive analytical review.

B442 Dixon, John W., Jr. "Voice of Ecstacy." Christian Century, LXXXVII (June 17, 1970), 761-762.
The reviewer comments on the theme: "To go to Jerusalem is to go home." He calls the book one of the most beautiful he has ever read. "Only the Jews in our day speak with such a voice, the voice of ecstacy, in the will of God. The cruelty of Christendom helped form such a voice in pain."

B443 Edelman, Lily. "A Jewish Book: What Is It?" National Jewish Monthly, LXXIX (January 1970), 49, 50.
"Elie Wiesel emerges as the contemporary Jewish writer who has turned Jewish defeat into triumph and Jewish suffering into eternal life."

B444 Elkin, Lillian. Jewish Frontier, XXXVII (May 1970), 34-36.
The greatest strength of the book the reviewer feels is the merging of reality and fantasy.

B445 Enright, D. J. London Magazine, X (October 1970), 88.
A strongly worded negative review. The tone throughout is called "so pretentious and portentous," the writing is referred to as "larded with meaningless mysteries and ill-timed or ill-judged aphorisms." The result is "credibility fails, and fortunately the reader is excused from the attempt, hardly seemly in a non-Jew, to assess the loss and gain as the Jews come home and put down the Torah for the sten-gun." The award of the Prix Medicis must have been motivated, according to this critic, "by feelings of guilt or sympathy rather than literary feelings."

B446 Erdosi, Elizabeth. "Paperbacks." Publishers Weekly, CXCVII (December 14, 1970), 40. (A review of the Avon Paperback)
"The novel is a profound spiritual adventure, and the Jew is a metaphor as well as a realistic character." Mention is made of the Prix Medicis and Book of the Month Club selection.

B447 *Fort Worth (Tex.) Press, February 22, 1970.
Some of the author's ideas are said to be cryptic and mystical, but his language is called superb.

B448 Freedman, Janet S. Library Journal, XCV (January 1, 1970), 84.
"This volume and all the author's work is exceptional for its philosophic content and moral earnestness."

B449 Friend, James. "The Curse of Survival in Life's Nightmare." Chicago Daily News, February 7, 1970, "Panorama" Sec., p. 11.
The theme of the meaninglessness of life and death is traced in Milton's Paradise Lost, as well as in Beggar in Jerusalem. The reviewer says of B. in J., "at the beginning of the 1970's it is certain to be one of the great books of the decade, perhaps of our entire woebegotten century." He goes on to say: "Like the Wailing Wall itself, it [B. in J.] is a monument to all men's suffering, to each man's need."

B450 Frisch, D. R. Minneapolis American Jewish World, February 13, 1970, p. 9.
The real hero of B. in J. is world Jewry, says this reviewer. "Wiesel's tale is of the Jew rediscovering himself."

B451 Garioch, Robert. "Wars." The Listener (London), LXXIV (July 23, 1970), 124.
"The whole of Jewish history is the time scale of which the Wall is a nearly timeless symbol."

B452 German, Art. "A Novel Not to Enjoy: A Madman's Witness." Sacramento Bee, March 1, 1970, p. 25.
Wiesel's beggar may claim to be a madman, but this reviewer says that it may well be that he makes more sense than most of the sane people in the world.

B453 Gregory, Marian Gavin. "Novel Covers Wealth of Jewish Experience." Fort Worth (Tex.) Morning Star Telegram, March 29, 1970, Sec. G, p. 8.
A brief abstract.

B454 Haddock, Louise. "Prize Novel of Israel." Tulsa (Okla.) World, April 19, 1970, Sec. E, p. 23.
The book is said to lead the reader into a dream

world of spiritual adventure, only to be suddenly awakened by the terrible sounds of war.

B455 Hill, William. America, CXXII (May 2, 1970), 478-479.
"Not everybody's cup of tea, this strangely evocative non-novel is about the beggars who are Jerusalem and embody Jewish history."

B456 Honolulu Star Bulletin, March 1, 1970, TV Aloha Magazine Sec., p. 27.
A brief, descriptive review.

B457 "Hour by Hour." Times Literary Supplement, October 9, 1970, p. 1172.
The reviewer calls the style of the book "a combining of dream-like fusion of meetings, personal stories and memories." The technique of having the narrator put himself through the eternal and universal experience of Jews, appears to this reviewer to be a connection falsely insisted upon.

B458 Isaac, Dan. "All My Stories Are True." The Nation, CCX (March 16, 1970), 309-310.
A positive analytical review. "A great work, this book of recollection is a holy act: the fulfilling of a uniquely felt religious commandment."

B459 Jordan, Clive. "Bearing Witness." New Statesman, LXXX (July 24, 1970), 95-96.
The reviewer says that Israel is now in its heroic period after the Six Day War and an emerging heroic literature will be forthcoming. He feels B. in J. qualifies because "it takes account of the nature of Jewish history, which has taught that survival is more practicable than supremacy." He calls the book an essentially Jewish chanson de geste like the Song of Roland. The function of Jerusalem's beggars he feels, is not to fight, but to bear witness to the continuous Jewish experience. The best part of the book is "the responsibility to experience."

B460 Kaplan, Howard M. "Powerful Tale of Six Day War: Mankind." Denver Post, February 1, 1970, "Roundup" Sec., p. 32.
Mr. Kaplan notes the tasteful presentation of the religious and the irreligious feelings of the men, and

says "Beggar in Jerusalem well may be one of the top literary works of 1970."

B461 Katz, Adolph. "The Will to Survive, Judaism's Spirit and Its Enemies." Philadelphia Bulletin, May 31, 1970, Sec. 2, p. 3.
The flashback technique used in the novel is discussed--this is a highly complimentary review.

B462 Kent, Harvey. Keeping Posted, XV (May 1970), 10. (A publication of the Union of American Hebrew Congregations for young people.)
An illuminating review by a twelfth-grader. His comments include: "It is an unsettling book about the history of the Jewish people and their fate. I would recommend it to anyone who has read a good deal about the factual aspects of the Holocaust and of the detailed methods of the calculated extermination of six million Jews. After you've read the facts, awaken the feelings. Read Beggar in Jerusalem. It makes you feel very Jewish."

B463 Kirsch, Robert. "Jerusalem Holds Promise of Peace." Los Angeles Times, March 22, 1970, "Calendar" Sec., p. 46.
More comment on the survival theme appears in this review. Jerusalem, a city that no one can enter and go away unchanged, is discussed. Finally, the idea of no safe and final answers is spoken about.

B464 Kolbert, Jack. "Wiesel Novel Is Termed Meritorious." Albuquerque Journal, May 18, 1970, Sec. A, p. 9.
"For the non-Jewish world, the novel is pregnant with some bitter truths which ring forth in pithy blade-like aphorisms.... Kill a Jew and you make him immortal."

B465 Langer, Lawrence. Woman's American Ort Reporter, XXI (March/April 1970), 4.
The intention of the book is said "to create a consciousness that life has thus far frustrated."

B466 Leonard, John. "History Has Bad Dreams." New York Times, January 27, 1970, p. 41.
"In six novels in four tongues, Mr. Wiesel has sought to discharge the burden of his witness." In commenting on the quality of Wiesel's writing, Mr.

Leonard continues: "so charged, so subtle, so superb is Mr. Wiesel's prose style, so dangerously lucid, that his memory becomes our reality; we wake up obliged to live his bad dream, as beggars asking for an innocence we never earned." Reprinted: Nashville Tennessean, February 15, 1970, Sec. A, p. 19.

B467 Leviant, Curt. "Elie Wiesel: A Soul on Fire." Saturday Review, LIII (January 31, 1970), 25-28.
An essay review of B. in J. and an excellent in-depth review of all of Wiesel's work. "After we have listened to what Wiesel has to say, other literature seems meaningless."

B468 *Long Beach (Cal.) Press Telegram, April 1, 1970.
Wiesel is called a novelist who really is a poet. Reprinted: *Long Beach (Cal.) Independent, April 12, 1970.

B469 McPherson, William. "How Does One Grasp the Holocaust." Washington Post, February 6, 1970, Sec. B, pp. 1, 12.
An excellent in-depth analytical review which comments on the Job theme and the author telling the tale and asking the questions. "Like Jerzy Kosinski, whose style is similar, Elie Wiesel has a way of sneaking up on horror and rendering it shockingly fresh." The reviewer says that some novels have to be pried open to yield their secrets, and that B. in J. is one of these. "Its best moments achieve tremendous power." Reprinted: *Springfield (Mass.) Republican, February 22, 1970; *Staten Island (N.Y.) Advance, March 16, 1970.

B470 Malin, Irving. "Wiesel's Prophetic Riddle." Congress Bi-Weekly, XXXVII (April 17, 1970), 17-18.
The reviewer raises many questions about the style of the book, but nevertheless concludes that the book is prophetic and brilliant.

B471 Manaster, Jane. "Six-Day War." Austin (Tex.) American-Statesman, March 15, 1970, Show World Sec., p. 28.
A brief review.

B472 Margolies, Rabbi Morris M. "For Hearts Singed by Suffering." Kansas City (Mo.) Star, January 25,

1970, Sec. D, p. 3.
An analysis of the beggar in the book is the feature of this review.

B473 Marsh, Peter. "In Search of Jerusalem." World Jewry, XIV (September 1971), 19.
"Wiesel is a living link between the Hasidic Kingdom of the Carpathians and the regenerated Jewish world of Israel."

B474 Murray, Shirley K. "The Mystique of Victory." Louisville Courier-Journal, March 22, 1970, Sec. F, p. 4.
The review deals with Wiesel's questioning technique.

B475 Myles, Naomi. "Centuries Telescope at the Wailing Wall." Charlotte (N.C.) Observer, February 8, 1970, Sec. F, p. 5.
The Six Day War as seen in the context of the Jewish experience is the theme Mrs. Myles deals with in her review.

B476 Nashville Tennessean, June 7, 1970, Sec. F, p. 10.
A brief, descriptive review.

B477 Negri, Sam. "In the Shadow of the Wall." New Haven Register, March 1, 1970, Sec. D, p. 4.
The best part of the book is the recapturing of the Old City.

B478 New Yorker, XLVI (June 6, 1970), 134.
"The theme is eternal Jewish suffering, and the result is a novel as a series of hysterical declamations, full of spurious profundities."

B479 *"Novel Searing in Intensity." Des Moines Tribune, February 19, 1970.
Review is reprinted from other sources.

B480 "Novel Reflects on Humanity." St. Petersburg Times, February 22, 1970, Sec. G, p. 5.
"After you have read a novel by Elie Wiesel, you feel you have read something important." The survival theme is touched upon.

B481 Oregonian (Portland), February 22, 1970, Sec. F, p. 6.

"A prize winner and best seller in France, this will be one of the most memorable novels published in America in 1970."

B482 "Out of Silence Toward Life." Time, XCV (March 16, 1970), 98.
"The great achievement of B. in J. is that Wiesel has shaped a story that shows men during a modern war, yet does justice to the brooding silences in which all violent action and its consequences are pondered and perhaps judged."

B483 Porterfield, Waldon R. "Ages Past and to Come Join at the Wailing Wall." Milwaukee Journal, February 8, 1970, Sec. 5, p. 4.
The enormous scope of the book is commented on by Mr. Porterfield. He calls B. in J. an "eloquent, wise and vehemently emotioned book by a writer of stature."

B484 Potok, Chaim. "Victims of the 'Holy' Madness." Newark Sunday Star Ledger, January 25, 1970, Sec. 4, p. 8.
A discussion of the beggars and their madness appears in this review. B. in J. is called a fascinating tale, establishing Wiesel as a major novelist. "It is also a testament to the living and the dead, and a luminous private vision of the heaven and hell we make of our lives here on earth." Reprinted: New York Post, January 26, 1970, p. 16; San Francisco Examiner, February 5, 1970, p. 31.

B485 Pritchett, V. S. "Ghosts." New York Review of Books, XLV (May 7, 1970), 10-12 [12]. (Appears with reviews of I. B. Singer's books.)
In comparison to Singer, "Wiesel is several removes from the primitive Jewish story-teller; or rather the story-teller is overlaid by the sophisticated impressionist." Mr. Pritchett calls the book one which is "perilously suspended between the noveau roman and the new Jewish Psalm. Wiesel is at his best in his power to move us with sharp fragments of Jewish history."

B486 Ridley, Clifford A. "Wiesel's Beggar Is a Wise Book and For the Ages." National Observer, IX (February 2, 1970), 19.

B. in J. is called a "prismatic novel, reflecting the dialogues of man, God and history in a thousand facts, in uncluttered prose that gleams again and again with the metaphor of the poet."

B487 Riemer, Jack. "Wiesel's World: The Horror and the Glory." Hadassah Magazine, LX (January 1970), 16-18.

Comments on the strength of the book. It lies in Wiesel's effort to express the wonder of the Six Day War.

B488 Rosenberg, Joseph. "Compelling Tale of Near-East War." Newark Daily News, June 14, 1970, sec. 6E, p. 22.

Mr. Rosenberg says that Wiesel has taken the stand of a modern-day prophet, calling on the people of Israel to follow the paths of righteousness dictated in God's law.

B489 Rosenbloom, Joseph R. "Transitional Jew." St. Louis Post Dispatch, January 25, 1970, Sec. C, p. 4.

"Elie Wiesel is the bleeding soul of the Holocaust." The reviewer feels that although the book is not as smoothly written as his early novels, "it is a testimony of the ambiguity of a Jew living in two psychological worlds."

B490 Rosenfeld, Ruth. "An Unhealed Wound." Houston Post, April 26, 1970, "Spotlight" Sec., p. 7.

The reviewer speaks of the use of stream of consciousness writing and of the wealth of tales and legends. She says "there is no way to define what is reality and what is imagined."

B491 Rubin, Lois Elinoff. "Wiesel Weaves Past into Future." Jewish Chronicle (Pittsburgh), April 30, 1970, p. 11.

"The weaving of so many historical patterns culminating in Israel's victory of 1967, gives a positive ending to the evolution of his [Wiesel's] literature of the Holocaust."

B492 Sanders, Nicholas. "Modern Jewish Life and Universal Concerns." Nashville Banner, February 20, 1970, p. 28.

The reviewer says that the style of the book veers from novelistic to reportorial with an occasional sortie into a dream-like poetic stance. "It is mainly the character of David, the beggar, the dreamer, the philosopher, who best expresses the universal concerns of the author and his place in the scheme of modern Jewish life."

B493 Schiff, Pearl. "Novel Blends Jewish Travail." Boston Morning Globe, February 26, 1970, p. 28.
"All the events of the past come together in a kind of spiritual ingathering to explain a modern miracle, Israel's Six Day War."

B494 Short, Kathryn S. "Novelist Explores Many Themes." Baton Rouge Advocate, June 14, 1970, Sec. F, p. 2.
The reviewer comments on the following themes of the novel: (1) life passed on from an elder to a youth--a form of eternal life; (2) "each man contains all"; (3) man's kinship to man; (4) difficulty of expressing God with words.

B495 Sneider, Marion. "Probing the Roots: the Jewish Riddle." Miami Herald, April 12, 1970, Sec. H, p. 7.
"beautiful simple poetic prose."

B496 Sperber, Manes. New York Times Book Review, January 25, 1970, pp. 1, 34.
The reviewer, a French writer, says that French critics and readers alike consider B. in J. Wiesel's finest work. "One of those rare literary achievements in which a writer succeeds in mastering a theme which has been dominating him for years." The reviewer feels that the man and his shadow will finally become one, "just as the ancient people and the young Israeli nation may become one."

B497 Stadtler, Bea. Jewish Education, XLII (Winter 1972-1973), 46.
The interview with Mota Gur is singled out as "priceless."

B498 *Stein, Kenneth E. "Bearers of Human History." Worcester (Mass.) Telegram, February 22, 1970.
A positive, analytical review.

B499 Stern, Daniel. "A Metaphor for Man." Chicago Tribune Book World, January 18, 1970, pp. 1, 3.
"A spiritual adventure so profound that it demands to be judged in terms of major world literature. Wiesel has taken the Jew as his metaphor--and his reality--in order to unite a moral and aesthetic vision in terms of all men."

B500 Subotnik, Norman. "Not to Be Explained." Baltimore Sun, April 12, 1970, Sec. D, p. 6.
"The wanderer and the beggar have their place in Jewish lore."

B501 Thompson, Francis J. "A Masterpiece of a Case History." Tampa Tribune, April 26, 1970, Sec. C, p. 5.
Wiesel's flash-back technique is discussed here.

B502 Thorpe, Day. Washington Star, February 8, 1970, Sec. 9, p. 2.
The reviewer says that few books are so inseparable an amalgam of autobiography and fiction as B. in J. is. He continues by saying that, of all the books he has read on the horror of the Jewish extermination, none seems as powerful as this one, where "the effect is created not by multiplication of sickening detail, but by Wiesel's talent in giving the impression, as though from the depths of a trance, that it is not a question of the Wandering Jew but of all mankind. We are all of us both murderer and victim."

B503 Weisman, John. "Novel Affirms Jewish Tradition." Los Angeles Times, April 19, 1970, "Book Review" Sec., p. 2.
The reviewer says that the style of B. in J. bears a more striking resemblance to Camus or Malraux rather than to Bellow or even I. B. Singer.

B504 Werry, Richard R. "The Past--Good or Evil--Is Inescapable." Detroit Daily News, February 22, 1970, Sec. E, p. 5.
Mr. Werry says of the novel that "it may be described as an impressionistic depiction of the Jewish consciousness in a time when the grandeur that was Israel under King David is being remembered and honored by a new generation which has installed a reign of physical courage and ethical pragmatism."

B505 Woestendick, Jo. "A Beggar's Eye Looks at Hate and the Holocaust." Houston Chronicle, March 1, 1970, p. 16.
"Wiesel takes his reader by the hand to the edge of insanity to questions that are gnawing, staggering."

B506 Wohlgelernter, Maurice. "The Beggar's Return." American Zionist, LX (May 1970), 39-41.
The author and the beggar become one, this reviewer feels, and as a seer he seeks the unity of the man and his shadow.

B507 Wolff, Geoffrey. "The Unspeakable." Newsweek, LXXV (February 9, 1970), 88, 92.
"B. in J. is neither a war novel nor the history of a nation. It seeks, through myth, aphorism, metaphysical speculation, conundrum, and time across centuries, to become a legend of the Jews, with the force and dimension of epic recapitulation."

B508 Young, Sonia. "Timely Today." Chattanooga (Tenn.) Times, March 8, 1970, Sec. B, p. 4.
The book is said to be beautifully written, imbued with symbolism and a poetic prose that makes it a major literary work.

ONE GENERATION AFTER

B509 Brady, Charles A. "After One Generation: An Extended Meditation." Buffalo Evening News, December 26, 1970, Sec. B, p. 8.
The reviewer feels that Wiesel should go on to other themes.

B510 *Broch, Nathan. "Views of Plight of Soviet Jewry." Houston Chronicle, December 26, 1971.
"If there is any wholeness in the stark fragmentation of Elie Wiesel's One Generation After, it is, perhaps, the nagging vision of death in progress."

B511 Cargas, Harry J. America, CXXIV (February 27, 1971), 210.
The reviewer says that Wiesel here, just as in his significant novels, records more than sorrow. "He presents the history of humanity." Overtones of Camus and Beckett in Wiesel's writing are mentioned.

B512 *Chandler, Harriette L. Worcester (Mass.) Telegram, November 22, 1970.
Comments on the autobiographical nature of the book are featured here.

B513 David, Gunter. "A Call to Remember from Elie Wiesel." Newark News, January 31, 1971, Sec. 6E, p. 18.
The terrifying message from this book is: "Was all the slaughter in vain? Has man learned nothing from the past?"

B514 Elkin, Lillian. "If I Still Scream." Congress Bi-Weekly, XXXVIII (June 18, 1971), 21-22.
"O.G.A. continues to explore, to recall and painfully reevaluate the events of the last twenty-five years.... Young readers revere Wiesel, for his ability to translate the particular into the universal."

B515 Farah, Ceasar E. "Anguished Plea That We Face the Dead Again." Minneapolis Tribune, February 14, 1971, Sec. E, pp. 10-11.
An analytical essay-review of the individual stories.

B516 Freedman, Janet. Library Journal, XCV (November 1, 1970), 3779.
"An outstanding book for all libraries."

B517 Friedlander, Albert H. Saturday Review, LIII (November 21, 1970), 40.
Mr. Friedlander calls the essays in this collection sparse, and says that in some ways it does not have the sweep of Wiesel's great novels, nevertheless "its very incompleteness becomes a communication."

B518 Halperin, Irving. "A Strong Voice Muffled in the Silence." San Francisco Examiner-Chronicle, January 31, 1971, "This World" Sec., p. 33.
In speaking of Wiesel, Mr. Halperin notes: "It is true that his voice is muffled by the realm of silence and shadows into which, one generation after, Auschwitz has receded. Still, he, [Wiesel] more than any other living writer on the Holocaust, momentarily tears open chinks in the silence with the force of his writing."

B519 Justice, John. "The Condition of the Jews." Greens-

boro (N.C.) Daily News, December 13, 1970, Sec. B, p. 3.
With acerbity Mr. Justice notes, "this troubling book is unlikely to reach many readers because it does not deal in the soporific cliches about Jews."

B520 Kaplan, Howard M. "Horror of Nazis Rekindled in 'Generation.'" Denver Post, December 20, 1970, "Roundup" Sec., p. 16.
Individual review of stories contained in this review. "The End of A Revolutionary" is singled out as most symbolic and parable-like.

B521 Lask, Thomas. "The Stain That Won't Go Away." New York Times, December 15, 1970, p. 43.
Mr. Lask calls Elie Wiesel a powerful and articulate defender of the new state of Israel.

B522 Lottman, Eileen. "Paperbacks." Publishers Weekly, CCI (January 24, 1972), 65.
A review of the Bard/Avon paperback. Wiesel's eloquence highly complimented.

B523 Maeroff, Gene I. "The Jewish Soul." Cleveland Plain Dealer, November 15, 1970, Sec. 7, p. 1.
What are of greatest interest to this reviewer are the stories directed to the young Jew of today and those to the New Left.

B524 Margolies, Rabbi Morris B. Kansas City (Mo.) Star, November 22, 1970, p. 30.
The story "Bar Mitzvah Watch" is singled out for specific critical examination.

B525 Marsh, Peter. "Witness for Humanity." World Jewry, XIV (August 1971), 20-21.
"Wiesel's style and presentation lifts his book far above the level of reportage. It is not German evil that sears Wiesel's soul but Man's evil. The essay "To a Young Jew of Today," is cited especially.

B526 Murray, Shirley K. "Elie Wiesel Collection: Essays and Musings." Louisville Courier-Journal, January 10, 1971, Sec. E, p. 5.
"The Six Day War now brings new witnesses to the mystery of Jewish survival."

B527 Myles, Naomi. "Haunted by Israel, Auschwitz." Charlotte (N.C.) Observer, April 4, 1971, Sec. F, p. 8.

The reviewer comments on Wiesel's refutation of the New Left.

B528 Plotkin, Rabbi Albert. Arizona Republic (Phoenix) March 28, 1971, Sec. N, p. 9.

A descriptive review. "The Bar Mitzvah Watch" discussed.

B529 Portrait, Ruth. "Auschwitz and the Astronauts." Jewish Observer and Middle East Review (London), XX (July 2, 1971), 18.

The reviewer finds Wiesel's statement that he will now go on to other than Holocaust themes difficult to imagine; "... with an author so obsessed with his theme, it is hard to believe such a statement."

B530 Potok, Chaim. "Despair and Hope Surviving the Worst Hells Created by Man." Chicago Sun-Times, November 29, 1970, "Book Week" Section, p. 16.

In speaking of Wiesel's soul, Mr. Potok says, "it is one that refuses to give way to ultimate despair, despite the blood and the fire, the indifference and the hopelessness."

B531 Riemer, Jack. "Wiesel Finds a New Concept of Sanity." Hadassah Magazine, LII (November 1970), 22-23.

"What Elie Wiesel has done in this book is to tell how Jews in the concentration camps, in Israel and in Russia, have given mankind a new definition of sanity, quite different from the commonly accepted concept."

B532 Schiller, Mordechai. "Poets and Madmen." Jewish Life (New York), XXXIX (April 1972), 55-59.

O.G.A. is reviewed along with Star Eternal by Katzetnik. The publication, which is an organ of the Union of Orthodox Jewish Congregations of America, presents a traditionalist viewpoint. The essay cited here is religious oriented with much rabbinic scholarship. The reviewer chides Wiesel for his non-religious ideas on Jewish destiny.

B533 Sherman, Ruth. "Book Mark." U.P.T.A. News (Board of Jewish Education, Inc.), VI (February

1973), 12.
"This is a novel in the finest sense, providing an emotional experience that becomes part of the reader. It shows a life-orientation well worth the close attention of all of us as individuals and as a people."

B534 "The Shock of Auschwitz." Times Literary Supplement (London), July 9, 1971, p. 809.
The reviewer finds that those stories that deal with holocaust remembrances are of excellent quality and are well written, citing the title essay and "The Bar Mitzvah Watch" as examples. Those essays that are on the subject of the Six Day War, however, he feels may have been good journalism a few days after the events, "but hardly stand up to reprinting in book form."

B535 Silver, Eric. "Obsession." Manchester Guardian, June 24, 1971, p. 9.
"Wiesel's special achievement is a perspective on the holocaust that relates it to the anguish of the Seventies." The critic says that he will press the book on his children as soon as they are old enough to understand it.

B536 Srouji, Jacque. "Mankind Asked to Stop Listen." Nashville Tennessean, January 24, 1971, Sec. F, p. 8.
"The beautiful thing about Elie Wiesel is that he never tires of shouting, asking mankind to stop and listen."

B537 Stern, Daniel. "Visions from the Holocaust." Chicago Tribune Book World, December 13, 1970, p. 4.
In a detailed analytical review of the individual stories, Mr. Stern says, "The Jew and the artist come together in these extraordinary pages."

B538 Subotnik, Norman. "A Nation That Made Murder Its Work." Baltimore Sun, December 27, 1970, Sec. D, p. 7.
Individual comment on the stories appears in this review.

B539 Walsh, Anne C. Phoenix (Ariz.) Gazette, November 28, 1970, pp. 20-21.
In an analytical review, the theme of presenting

questions and not answers is explored.

B540 Wohlgelernter, Maurice. "From Generation to Generation: Or Elie Wiesel's Oral and Written Tradition." Tradition, XI (Spring 1971), 105-120 [109-120].
The reviewer comments on the immense popularity of Elie Wiesel as a lecturer in his YMHA series at 92nd Street, N.Y.C. "He transmits orally as well as in his writing his haunting concern for Jewish survival."

B541 Women's American ORT Reporter, XXI (November/December 1970), 10.
A brief, descriptive review.

SOULS ON FIRE

B542 Ages, Arnold. "In Marvellous Cadence. And Joy. And Fervor." Toronto Globe and Mail, March 25, 1972, p. 33.
A comprehensive review, citing Hasidic background material. "Elie Wiesel has done a service to the Jewish people, and to humanity for sensitizing us to those gentle masters. His is the soul on fire."

B543 Arden, Doren. "Of Moral Strength and Old Traditions." Detroit News, March 26, 1972, Sec. E, p. 5.
Praises the book as an inspiration, but the reviewer notes sadly that the author presumes a great deal of preliminary knowledge of Jewish history and customs from his readers and that "Souls on Fire is not a book which will be easily accessible to non-Jews or even to Jews who have lost touch with their traditions."

B544 Bandler, Michael J. "A Nostalgic Glimpse at Hasidism." Commonweal, XCVI (April 28, 1972), 194-196.
Many excerpts from the book are given along with much background material on Hasidism. In his analytical comments, Mr. Bandler calls S. on F. a towering inspiring document of faith in man's inexplicable, yet unwavering capacity to begin again. It is also renewed proof, though, that Elie Wiesel will never forget the past that we ultimately share.

B545 Berger, Alan L. "The Sources of Hasidic Experience." Midstream, XIX (February 1973), 77-79.
Though the reviewer notes that S. on F. is the most "hopeful" of Wiesel's works, his [Wiesel's] existential philosophy requires him to include the Holocaust. "Wiesel's existential angst has led him back to the Hasidic tales he heard as a child." The success of the book lies in its ability to convey to the reader "a feeling for the vitality and impact of the Zaddikim. Wiesel is a gifted artist whose subject has clearly touched him, as well as having been touched by him."

B546 Bermant, Chaim. London Jewish Chronicle, December 15, 1972, p. 12.
The written material is compared to the telling of the tales by Wiesel at the 92nd St. "Y". He feels that "the tales removed from the teller lose something of their magic. He wonders how Wiesel could have recounted them all on paper without some sort of critical intrusion."

B547 Bloom, Albert W. "Holocaust ... Whose Souls on Fire?" Pittsburgh Jewish Chronicle, November 23, 1972, p. 16.
An essay-review of the book. Much interest in Hasidism today noted. The review appears in connection with a lecture by Mr. Wiesel at the B'nai Israel Synagogue in Pittsburgh.

B548 "Book Draws From Hasidic Masters." Los Angeles Times, February 20, 1972, Sec. F, p. 13.
A summary type review.

B549 Buchstein, Fred. "Hasidic Prayers Are Wiesel-Worded." Cleveland Press, March 10, 1972, Showtime Sec., p. 20.
Wiesel's scope is spoken of here. He is said to be doing more in the book than just recalling Hasidic legends. "He is praying at a time when the minds of many men are closed to God." The reviewer concludes with the hope: "We can only pray that Wiesel's prayers are heeded by other men." Reprinted: *Baltimore News-American, March 19, 1972.

B550 Booklist, LXVIII (June 15, 1972), 869.
S. on F. is called "thematically universal."

B551 Books and Bookmen, XVIII (January 1973), 122.
A short summary review.

B552 "Burning." Kansas City (Mo.) National Catholic Reporter, March 17, 1972, p. 18.
A short comment.

B553 Cox, Harvey. "Critic's Choices." Commonweal, XCVII (February 23, 1973), 477.
One of a variety of books that Mr. Cox includes in his selections for "Religious Book Week."
"After so many books about religion, it is good to get back to the ding an sich, and that is why Elie Wiesel's S. on F. with its masterful retelling of the yarns of the Hasidic masters appealed to me so much. I hope Wiesel's example will be followed and we will get more collections like this, wound together with just enough narrative and history to place the stories themselves in their proper setting."

B554 Cunneen, Sally. "Critics Choice for Christmas." Commonweal, XCVII (December 8, 1972), 234.
A positive descriptive review.

B555 Davis, Bob. "Old Credo Still Has Much To Say." Santa Rosa (Cal.) Press Democrat, March 26, 1972, p. 33.
The book is termed a "nostalgia trip" for Wiesel. The concept of shekina in Hasidism is dealt with. Buber, Emerson are listed as extra-religious influences on the author. Wiesel is credited with successfully capturing the charismatic quality of the Hasidic leaders.

B556 Dobbs, Kildare. "New Book a Beautiful Poem On Masters of Jewish Sect." Toronto Star, March 1, 1972, p. 54.
After giving much background material on Hasidism, this reviewer states: "Readers brought up in the Christian tradition may envy these Jews their hope, their patience." His evaluation of the author is equally as glowing: "It is impossible not to be moved by Wiesel's book. The great rabbis are still radiant with life in his imagination, and he writes of them not as a historian or theologian but as a poet."

B557 Duhamel, P. Albert. Boston Herald-Traveler, March

5, 1972, Sec. 8, p. 12.
In a lengthy in-depth review, the following comment on Wiesel is made: "His portraits make intelligible--and accessible to a broad public for the first time--some of the forces which kept the chosen people together right through the holocaust."

B558 Edelman, Lily. "Opening the Hasidic Gates." National Jewish Monthly, LXXXVI (March 1972), 72-77.
A comprehensive account of the individual Tzaddikim featured in the book, pointing out their particular charismatic qualities. An insert taken from the book called "Sparklets from Souls on Fire," is included. Mrs. Edelman's comments include: "In a world sadly devoid of brightness or affirmation, Wiesel's retelling of his favorite Hasidic tales has the power to warm our hearts and recharge our spiritual batteries."

B559 "Encounters with the Masters." Times Literary Supplement, June 29, 1973, p. 755.
Wiesel's personal approach to Hasidism is scored as compared to other more objective erudite studies.

B560 Evett, Robert. "Loving Portraits of Souls on Fire." Washington Star, March 6, 1972, Sec. A, p. 11.
"Wiesel has done a superb and loving job of presenting the history of and the case for Hasidism. His is one of the few books on religion I know that demands absolutely no concessions from the reader, but he does point out that one refuses nothing to a Baal Shem."

B561 Feldman, Garrick. "Telling Dreams and Stories to Survive." Chicago Sun-Times, February 27, 1972, Showcase Sec., p. 18.
A mainly explanatory treatment of Hasidism, in which the tales are said to have one common characteristic: "they teach decency, but none inspires listeners to shake the world."
[A letter to the editor, concerning this review appeared in the Chicago Sun-Times on March 12, 1972, by Shirley Feldman of Sterling, Illinois. She states that the reviewer does a grave injustice to a valiant people by stating in his review that millions of Jews walked to the Nazi gas chambers with no resistance.]

B562 Friedlander, Albert H. Saturday Review, LV (February 26, 1972), 76-77.

Wiesel is called one of the great story tellers of tales of our time in this complete review of the Hasidic tales.

B563 Garber, Frederick. "Sentimental Journey." Commentary, LIV (September 1972), 85-86.

In an essay review filled largely with negative criticism, Wiesel is faulted for lack of character in his book. Mr. Garber feels that the reader is left with only hearsay about the charisma that Wiesel says the Hasidim possessed and "with no living sense of that blazing power of intellect." He goes on to say that Wiesel uses sentimentalism to mean a "tendency to exploit the easier possibilities of the material." As the book progresses it is said to become vaguer and more shrill. "At its core is a large blur which belies its surface persuasiveness and the admirable intensity of its passion."

B564 Haramgaal, Yaaqov. "Gleanings from the Israeli Press." The American Zionist, LXII (June 1972), 30-32.

Excerpts are given from the various Israeli review of Souls on Fire, along with some interpretation. The article mainly quoted is by David Lazar. "Chasidut Al M'Pat Haolom" (Hasidism on the Map of the World) Mariv, March 14, 1972, p. 33. (B791)

B565 Hasden, Wes. "One Answer." Chattanooga (Tenn.) Times, May 7, 1972, Sec. F, p. 2.

"Existential; interesting, alive with legend and folklore, filled with stories repeated from generation to generation, this is a book that cries to be read for reasons other than mere entertainment, even though it provides ample amount of that all too rare commodity."

B566 Highet, Gilbert. Book-of-the-Month-Club News, April, 1972, pp. 8-9.

After a discussion of other books on the subject of Hasidism, Mr. Highet says that Wiesel's book is the first known to him to give a connected history of the Hasidic movement. "Elie Wiesel goes further into the psychology of the different Hasidic masters and makes them live again."

B567 Jacobson, David. "To Help Heal the Wounds of a Torn Generation." Jewish Welfare Board Circle In Jewish Bookland, November 1972, p. 1.
In a largely descriptive review, the story-telling abilities of Wiesel are noted.

B568 Johnston, Albert H. "Forecasts." Publishers Weekly, CCI (January 17, 1972), 52.
"This collection is sparked by the author's intense fervor and concise dramatic writing."

B569 Kahn, Lothar. "History of the Heart." Christian Century, LXXXIX (May 24, 1972), 609-610.
An in-depth essay. In the descriptive section, material from the book is used to tell of the Baal Shem Tov. Mrs. Wiesel's translation is said to catch the flavor of her husband's prose and "in its own manner ably calibrated the mood of the book." In speaking of the author, Mr. Kahn states that Hasidism has transformed Wiesel into an affirmationist. He wished to repay his debt to Hasidism by reconstructing its initially joyful, creative, communal phases. "This he has done with unparalleled skill and with a spirit and style that connote a joy, a creativity, and a communality that represent the inner life and teachings of souls on fire."

B570 Kellner, M. E. "The Jewish Book Shelf." Long Island (N.Y.) Jewish Press, February 1973, p. 39.
The book is referred to as a sensitive and warm evocation of a movement and its leaders. "Wiesel successfully treads the narrow line between dry sociology and uncritical romanticism."

B571 Kirkus, XXXIX (December 15, 1971), 1359.
A descriptive account of the tales is given. It is called "a revivifying collection."
"Throughout the tales of other great Masters Wiesel reenters a dazzling world of religious certainties and everything is possible."

B572 Kirsch, Robert R. "Legends of the Hasidic Masters." Los Angeles Times, March 29, 1972, Sec. 4, p. 20.
Comparison to Buber's ideology is made. Wiesel's own involvement in Hasidic thinking is what this reviewer feels is the key to the success of credibility

of ideas.

B573 Levy, Isaac. "Does Hasidism Have Any Relevance Today." Jewish Observer and Middle East Review (London), XXI (November 24, 1972), 24.
S. on F. is reviewed together with Hasidic Prayer by Louis Jacobs. Ideas on Messiah-consciousness are featured. In contrasting the two authors, the critic terms Wiesel a story-teller and Jacobs an academic analyst.

B574 Lottman, Eileen. "Paperbacks." Publishers Weekly, CCIII (January 15, 1973), 66.
A preview of the Vintage edition of S. of F.
"One can't help being impressed with the frequent similarities to philosophies and examples of daily life experiences in this collection and in the recently popularized Eastern religious tales."

B575 Malin, Irving. "Fire and Word." Congress Bi-Weekly, XXXIX (April 28, 1972), 26.
S. on F. is termed not an instant history nor a critical analysis of Hasidism. "He [Wiesel] hopes to plunge into the fire and by doing so, to transmit the glory of Hasidic fervor."

B576 Manaster, Jane. Austin (Tex.) American Statesman, June 18, 1972, Show-World Sec., p. 38.
A largely negative review. The critic loses her credibility by repeatedly referring to the book as Souls on Ice.

B577 Margolies, Morris B. "From the Shadow of Death." Kansas City (Mo.) Star, March 12, 1972, Sec. G, p. 3.
Much mention is made of the use of parable in the book. "Wiesel sees his mission as the retention of a semblance of sanity so as to be able to distinguish between the Kingdom of Light and the Kingdom of Darkness."

B578 *Marrus, Michael R. "Chasidic Response to Despair." The Canadian Jewish News, March 31, 1972.
The theme of the creative spark is enumerated in a lengthy essay-review of Hasidism.

B579 Marty, Martin E. "Religious Books." The Critic,

XXX (May/June 1972), 86.
Mr. Marty in a comprehensive review of many religious books says that S. on F. is "literally the most attractive book dealing with religion among those that have drawn my attention recently."

B580 ______. Commonweal, XCVII (February 23, 1973), 480.
"It is not Wiesel's own best book, but this survivor of the concentration camps takes the point of post-holocaust Judaism and looks back with favor on the Hasidic lore. Wit, reverence, coping, tragedy, learning, all are revealed in the story of these remarkable Jewish teachers."

B581 Mendel, Art. Jewish World of Long Island, October 27, 1972, p. 4.
"The real value of the book lies in the author's making the story of the Hasidic movement readily accessible to us and easily readable."

B582 Mohs, Mayo. "Voices Amid Thunder." Time, XCIX (May 3, 1972), 88.
The reviewer comments on the change in Wiesel's theme from the Holocaust in the last nine books to "religious joy, that mystical and ecstatic strain in Judaic history known as Hasidism." He calls the book "a stunning affirmation of life."

B583 Morlino, Robert C., S.J. Best Sellers, XXXII (April 1972), 37-38.
S. on F. is recommended very highly to the following three groups:
1) Anyone seeking a better understanding of religious experience.
2) Philosophers and theologians interested in engaging in a new perspective on religious experience and in "observing a marvellous usage of religious language."
3) Non-Jewish persons "in search of a deeper understanding and love of their Jewish brethren.

B584 Murray, Michele. "Hasidism is Alive: Reviving the Ancient Legends." National Catholic Reporter (Kansas City, Mo.), April 28, 1972, p. 15.
Hasidism as a movement is discussed, comments on Buber are made, along with mention of the inter-

disciplinary effects of the work. "Elie Wiesel has written a beautiful book that hints--only hints--at some of the treasures of Jewish spirituality that can enrich all people."

B585 Myles, Naomi. "Exposing the Roots of Hasidic Sect." Charlotte (N.C.) Observer, February 17, 1972, Sec. B, p. 8.
A descriptive review, citing aphorisms.

B586 New Yorker, XLVIII (April 15, 1972), 148.
A comparison of Hasidism to other movements within Christianity which have emphasis on inspiration rather than authority, is made, i.e. Quakerism, Quitism. The individuality of Hasidic rabbis who taught by example is further compared to the parables of the New Testament and the gnomic sayings of Zen.

B587 "New and Recommended." New York Times Book Review. March 19, 1972, p. 45.
"A gallery of the founders of Hasidic Jewry, brought glowingly to life, along with their philosophical tales and legends, reinterpreted existentially."

B588 Palm Springs (Cal.) Desert Sun. "Book News," September 26, 1972, Sec. A, p. 5.
In a short descriptive review, S. on F. is called "a book by one of the finest contemporary Jewish authors."

B589 Penn, Tobey. "With Perfect Faith, I Believe." Cleveland Jewish News, May 1, 1972, p. 21.
The basic tenets of Hasidism are explored. The "spark" as demonstrated by Wiesel is discussed.

B590 Potok, Chaim. "Out of Despair to Deepest Joy." Philadelphia Bulletin, March 5, 1972, Sec. 2, p. 3.
"Souls on Fire is Hasidism seen through the sensibility of one of the great writers of our time."

B591 Prescott, Peter S. "Talking to God." Newsweek, LXXIX (February 28, 1972), 88, 91.
Much explanation of the Hasidic movement is given. The book is called "an obligatory act of remembrance." Reprinted: Temple Beth Tikvah The Scroll, May 1972, p. 6.

B592 _______ and Clemons, Walter. "Readout: The Year in Books." Newsweek, LXXXI (January 1, 1973), 54.

In a listing of the best reading of '72 S. on F. is cited in comparison with David Halberstam's The Best and the Brightest as similar in the sense of personal involvement with the subject. Rated "eloquent."

B593 Pryce-Jones, Alan. Washington Post Book World, March 19, 1972, p. 12.

This reviewer feels that Wiesel stands too close to his subject, and as such he [Wiesel] gives the reader little more insight than a glossary and a synchronology.

B594 Putcamp, Luise, Jr. "Wiesel's 'Souls': A Special Kind of Mystic Jew." Columbia (S.C.) Record, May 21, 1972.

The Associated Press review which was reprinted in many places (see below) uses glib phrases in a glossy type critique. The book is said to contain "practical proverbs which can help people who can stand to be haunted a little." Reprinted: "Homilies from the Hasids: In Hell One Prays Better Than in Paradise." Middletown (Ohio) Journal, May 21, 1972, Entertainment sec., p. 52; "The Legends of Hasidic Jewry," Stockton (Cal.) Record, May 25, 1972, Focus sec., p. 6; "Who Are Hasids?" Berkeley (Cal.) Daily Gazette, May 27, 1972, Vista Views, p. 14; "A Little Haunted." Tulsa World, June 4, 1972, World Sec., p. 16; "Hasids: Special Kind of Jews." Birmingham (Ala.) News, June 4, 1972, sec. E, p. 7; *High Point (N.C.) Enterprise, June 4, 1972; "On Hasidic Masters." Merced (Cal.) Sun-Star, June 8, 1972, sec. 1, p. 8; "Bound to Be Read." Manchester (N.H.) News, June 11, 1972, p. 39; "On Hasidic Masters." Casa Grande (Ariz.) Dispatch, July 5, 1972, Sec. 1, p. 2; "Mystery Role of Hasidic Masters." Pasadena Star-News, July 16, 1972, Arts and Books Sec., p. 4; *Oxnard (Cal.) Press Courier, September 3, 1972; "Hasids are Termed Practical Mystics." Durham (N.C.) Herald, September 17, 1972, Sec. D, p. 5; *San Angelo (Tex.) Standard-Times, September 17, 1972.

B595 Rawick, A. J. Jewish Frontier, XXXIX (May 1972), 27-28.

The book is called a "mosaic" whose tone is "epic." "Today, Elie Wiesel has not only become transmitter of the Hasidic masters, but spokesman for man who is precariously balanced on the edge of the apocalyptic abyss."

Mr. Rawick speaks about Wiesel's existentialism, notes how he (unlike most others) negates the concept of the absurd. He focuses on Wiesel's idea that "man owes it to himself to reject despair." There is then no choice left. "One must impose a meaning on what perhaps has none and draw ecstasy from nameless faceless pain." The review shows how Hasidism has done this as chronicled by Wiesel.

B596 Riemer, Jack. "The Hassidic Masters: Portrayed by a Master." Hadassah Magazine, LIII (February 1972), 19-20.

Mr. Riemer states that the book not only tells that Hasidism once lived, but it demonstrates that it still does.

B597 Roskies, David M. The Jewish Quarterly (London), XX (Autumn 1972), 22-23.

Wiesel is called one of the most important Jewish novelists of our generation. The quality of the book is its "attempt to recreate a past and allow its vitality to infiltrate and modify our present understanding." A good analytical review.

B598 Siegel, Seymour. America, CXXVI (April 29, 1972), 467-8.

The role of Hasidism in the world today--"a unique source of inspiration and vitality"--is portrayed well in S. on F.

B599 Silberman, Charles E. "How to Live Joyously When There Are No Answers." New York Times Book Review, March 5, 1972, pp. 1, 26.

Wiesel is called in this in-depth essay-review "one of the great writers of this generation. Souls on Fire makes comparison with Camus inevitable." A review of the author's career is given outlining the themes and ideas that have been used in his literary career. His uniqueness in the past, when he dealt with Holocause themes, was his concern with life rather than death. Throughout that time, a connecting link ran through his work, the search for sanity in the face of insanity. Mr. Silberman feels that "S. on F. is the product of that search and the answer to it; it should be read by everyone concerned with the existential question, which is to say, by every sensitive and thinking human being." There is much example of Hasidic thinking given from the book focusing on the Hasidic way to live joyously. The reason for the great appeal of this philosophy in the 1970's is the quote the reviewer uses from the book: "Hasidism ... requires that every man share in every other man's life and not leave him to himself in either sorrow or joy."

B600 Smolar, Boris. "Between You and Me: Hasidism Magnet to Jewish Youth." The Jewish Community Voice, March 17, 1972, p. 7.
Much background material on the Lubavitcher movement is given. How will they welcome Wiesel's book --very warmly Mr. Smolar feels, because "Wiesel has the soul of a Hasid."

B601 ________. "Interest in Hasidism Greater than at Any Period of History." Denver Intermountain Jewish News, March 17, 1972, pp. 17, 27.
Uses the book as a focal point to cite the interest among youth in Hasidism. He points to the many courses on Hasidism that are offered at various Hillel chapters on college campuses around the country.

B602 Srouji, Jacque. "Haunting Continuity Hallmark of Wiesel." Nashville Tennessean, May 14, 1972, Sec. F, p. 14.
A laudatory review which comments on the author never giving up hope.

B603 Stern, Daniel. "The Master of the Good Name." The Nation, CCXIV (March 20, 1972), 379-380.
Much biographical background on Wiesel's own Hasidic background is given. Mrs. Wiesel's translation is noted especially as being done with great sensitivity.
S. on F. is said to have no pre-existing model. "It is not to be read as sociology, theology or the history of religion--though it is all of these. It is a novel written by history in which the characters are of towering stature: these Masters are wild men, sages, self-doubters, princes of pride. They embody every vice and virtue, but on a superhuman scale."

B604 Stuttaford, Genevieve. "Souls on Fire Tales of Hasi-

dism." San Francisco Examiner and Chronicle, February 27, 1972, This World Sec., p. 35.
In a review that also includes an interview with the author, the book is referred to "as a poetic book."

B605 Talmey, Allene. Vogue, CLIX (June 1972), 16.
"A God-struck book."

B606 Task, Arnold S. "A Truly Beautiful Book." Greensboro (N.C.) News, May 28, 1972, Sec. E, p. 3.
The spark of the Hasidic movement that Wiesel has captured is the focus for this positive review.

B607 Tuchman, Maurice. Library Journal, XCVII (March 1, 1972), 886.
A descriptive review.

B608 *Tujunga (Cal.) Record Ledger, February 17, 1963.
S. on F. is highly recommended for young readers.

B609 Ullian, Robert. Boston Phoenix, July 12, 1972, p. 17.
The theme of communing with a world that the author once knew, is stressed. S. on F. is termed "a weird heartbreaking volume."

B610 Weiss-Rosmarin, Trude. "Hasidic Tales." The Jewish Spectator, XXXVIII (April 1972), 7-8.
The quality of the book is the realization that when Wiesel finds himself in the teaching of the rebbies such as Israel of Rizshin, Lev-Yitzhak of Berditchev and Mendl of Kotzk "he does not recreate them in his image but finds himself in them." Reprinted: The Bridge (Sydney, Australia), August 1972, pp. 59-60.

B611 "Wiesel's Souls on Fire Enhances Traditions and Folklore of Hasidism." Detroit Jewish News, February 25, 1972, p. 25.
"In Souls on Fire we have another inspired work by the eminent author who has himself become the adherent to and the carrier of the messages of the master who carried inspiration into Jewish homes in many lands."

B612 Wohlgelernter, Maurice. The American Zionist, LXIII (September 1972), 38-40.
The individual masters are analyzed in this com-

prehensive essay. Particular emphasis is given to the treatment of Mendl of Kotzk, the virtues of revolt and defiance against God's "hiddeness" and man's inhumanity to man, and to himself.

NIGHT, DAWN, THE ACCIDENT: Three Tales by Elie Wiesel

B613 Brunsdale, Mitzi M. "First Three Works of One of This Generation's Greatest Writers." Houston Post, November 19, 1972, Spotlight Sec., p. 10.
Complimentary comments on all three books. The reviewer says that Wiesel's message throughout is that the survival of the camps would come to be more of a burden than death itself.

B614 *Conley, Andrea. "Trilogy: Two Novels and One True Story." Pittsboro (N.C.) Herald, November 5, 1972.
Good descriptive material given. The comment: "This is an excellent set of works to have been combined," is included. Reprinted: Augusta (Ga.) Chronicle-Herald, November 5, 1972, Sec. F, p. 12.

B615 "Death Throes." Times Literary Supplement, February 15, 1974, p. 49.
Comments on the overriding theme of death in the trilogy. Says that the best thing about the collection is "a close and profound engagement, in terms both religious and psychological, with the one subject that concerns us even more certainly than taxation."

B616 Gosnell, John S. "A Writer Who's Been There." Norfolk Virginian Pilot, February 4, 1973, Sec. C, p. 6.
The triptych as a whole is said to contain "some of the most moving prose in recent memory. The Accident is termed the least of the three in depth, but it "affords Wiesel some virtuoso passages."

B617 Greenstone, Maryann Dunitz. "One Man's Voyage to Hell." Detroit News, November 5, 1972, Sec. E, p. 5.
Complimentary comments made about all three of the books.

B618 Hunter, Larry. Portland (Ore.) Journal, October 21, 1972, Weekend Living Sec., p. 4.
Says that the trilogy should be proscribed reading for everyone. "Elie Wiesel is the wordsmith of wonderful ability and feeling."

B619 Levy, Henry W. "Elie Wiesel: The Man and the Writer." Pioneer Women, XLVIII (January 1973), 6-7.
Review essay on the trilogy. Background material on the author given in connection with an award given to Wiesel on behalf of the American Zionist movement.

B620 *Longstreet, Steven. Los Angeles Canyon Crier, October 9, 1972.
A brief summary.

B621 Parfet, Ione. Wichita Falls (Tex.) Times, December 31, 1972, Sunday Magazine Sec., p. 5.
Of the three books, The Accident is scored highest. It is called "the one which brings the deepest and most heartfelt sigh, for it highlights the blighting, destructive power of persistent memory upon man's life, his soul."

B622 Portland Oregonian, November 5, 1972, Sun-Day Sec., p. 25.
The connecting link among the novels is explored in this mainly descriptive review.

B623 Powers, Ed. "Wiesel: Words Among the Corpses." Cleveland Press, October 6, 1972, Showtime Sec., p. 18.
Wiesel is termed "low on inspiration but high on insight, though by personal example he refutes the contradiction.... While fellow captives drove themselves to inarticulate rage, Wiesel chose a poetic search for truths from which we may all benefit."

B624 Spurling, John. "Life Seen from the Outside." New Statesman, LXXXVII (February 1, 1974), 159.
The British edition of the trilogy is reviewed along with other current British books. "The documentary nature of Night, with its overwhelming content of hideous facts, pre-empts one's response to all three stories. If one were to assume that the other two were fiction and judge them only by what is written on the

page, they might appear somewhat crudely handled."

B625 Yohe, Susan. "His Life Was a Nightmare." Cincinnati Post and Times, November 25, 1972, Saturday Magazine Sec., p. 2.
A review written in retrospect after Souls on Fire.

THE OATH

B626 Abrahamson, Irving. "An Appointment with History." Chicago Sun-Times, November 18, 1973, Showcase Sec., p. 18.
"The Oath rejecting silence, is a call to life from the very center of death. It is a major work by a major writer."

B627 Bandler, Michael J. "A Jew On the Holocaust." Washington (D.C.) Star-News, December 18, 1973, Sec. C, p. 4.
In an in-depth review, Mr. Bandler speaks of the dire condition of the world, and how Wiesel feels that mankind has learned nothing of the Holocaust. He calls The Oath "Wiesel's most ambitious, most rewarding story to date, and one of his best books." The reviewer also delineates Wiesel's treatment of the holocaust in this book which is to confront by inference rather than directly.

B628 Bannon, Barbara A. Publishers Weekly, CCIV (October 1, 1973), 76.
Faults the book and Wiesel for trying to say too much. "Whatever the nightmares personal and shared lying behind this dark and painful story, they don't quite find fully articulate expression in it.... The Oath is haunting, but less for itself than for the historical nightmares that gave rise to it."

B629 *Berman, Michael L. Groton (Conn.) News, January 30, 1974.
This reviewer feels that loyal Wiesel readers will be in a quandry with The Oath. "It lacks the touch of wisdom and self-denial contained in the author's other works."

B630 Booklist, LXX (January 15, 1974), 518.
In a positive, mainly descriptive review, the book

is called demanding but rewarding reading.

B631 Boston Jewish Times, December 20, 1973, p. 15.
"Readers of The Oath will not be disappointed with Wiesel as a novelist."

B632 *Boulton, Joyce R. "Elie Wiesel's Novel Offers Positive View." Fort Worth (Tex.) Morning Star-Telegram, January 6, 1974.
The novel is said to offer a rational for life.

B633 Brady, Charles A. "Village That Vanished from Map, Memory." Buffalo (N.Y.) News, December 1, 1973, Sec. C, p. 8.
"Though not as exquisitely crafted as the best of Wiesel, The Oath is a resonant Kaddish of a book. If its theme is a somber one, its impact is not."

B634 Brin, Ruth F. "Wiesel's World: Destruction, Terror, and a Mystical Vision." Minneapolis Tribune, December 9, 1973, Sec. D, p. 9.
The Oath is scored for being a completely developed novel and not a collection of short sketches. Wiesel's struggle is caused by human suffering at the hands of other humans, this reviewer feels. She further states that the evil Wiesel speaks of must be recorded in order to be confronted. A very positive review.

B635 Bromwich, David. "A Novel Triumphs Over Bitter Logic." San Francisco Examiner, December 11, 1973, p. 30.
"Wiesel's novel stands precariously on the brink of literature, and in the end we can hardly fault it for caring about truth more than beauty: the truth, that is, not of the prophet Moshe, but of [Azriel] the old survivor." Reprinted: Book World, November 11, 1973, p. 12.

B636 Burlington (Vt.) Free Press, February 20, 1974, p. 26.
A positive descriptive review.

B637 *Burton, Hal. El Paso (Tex.) Times, December 30, 1973.
The ritual murder theme is explored.

B638 Cargas, Harry James. "A Terrible Vengeance of

Silence." St. Louis Post-Dispatch, November 11, 1973, Sec. B, p. 4.
Says The Oath is the first novel in which wholesale massacre is described. "It is a rare book where a soul is revealed."

B639 ______. America, CXXX (January 19, 1974), 41.
The Oath can rightly be included in Wiesel's twelve books, all of which "compose a magnificent mosaic of questions with eternal significance."

B640 Charleston (S.C.) News and Courier, December 30, 1973, Sec. D, p. 3.
"Story is dominated by haunted, end-of-the-world poetry."

B641 Cohen, George. "Wiesel's Survivors: At the End of Suffering-Gratitude." Chicago Tribune Book World, November 18, 1973, Sec. 7, p. 3.
"Wiesel has shown in The Oath how a small stupid incident can bring about a tragedy and that when we try to hurt others, we hurt ourselves. In his personal, poetic style he continues to be the most eloquent spokesman, not only for the Jews of silence but for the whole human race."

B642 Dome, Enid. "The Vital Connection." Congress Bi-Weekly, XLI (February 8, 1974), 18-19.
"A powerful statement about Jewish history and Jewish survival in a non-Jewish world."

B643 Fiske, Edward B. "Avenging Gods, Human Wolves." New York Times, January 16, 1974, p. 37.
The Oath is termed "vintage Wiesel." "The account of the actual physical attack in the closing pages is as vivid and alarming as anything he has ever written." Mr. Fiske says too, that The Oath goes beyond past treatment of similar themes. There is a new depth of pessimism he feels, and quoting from the Rebbe: "We were wrong.... [W]rong to try wrong to hope. Help cannot come from the other side. A Jew must not expect anything from man. Consolation can and must come only from God." The apocalyptic dimension of the novel is noted as well. "Elie Wiesel the story teller has become Elie Wiesel the prophet."
Reprinted: *Evansville (Ind.) Press, January 31,

1974; *Saskatoon (Kan.) Star-Phoenix, February 15, 1974; Winston Salem (N.C.) Journal and Sentinel, February 17, 1974, p. 4.

B644 Friedman, Alan. "Chronicle of a Pogrom." New York Times Book Review, November 18, 1973, pp. 5-6.

This reviewer finds the quality of the book uneven. The character of Moshe the Madman is called the great achievement of the book. "Still, the book as a whole resists Moshe and remains the ghost of a work that has been willed into motion by a historical pain so genuine, so insistantly close, that it can barely be forced to adopt the disguise of fiction."

B645 Friend, James. "Elie Wiesel's New Nightmare Journey." Chicago News, November 17, 1973, Panorama Sec., p. 12.

"As a storyteller, Wiesel has few peers in contemporary fiction. He is obsessively readable. As the conscience of our humanity, he is unique. In creating language as the omnipotent and atoning link between man and God, he, more than any other living writer, demands from his reader that sacrifice that comes from turning within one's self."

B646 Garber, Zev. Library Journal, XCIX (January 1, 1974), 68.

"A truly powerful novel, interwoven with threads of Hasidic tales, cabalistic mysticism, Talmudic sayings and pietistic folklore."

B647 Gelman, Ellen Gilbert. "Profoundly Moving Story." Worcester (Mass.) Telegram, December 2, 1973, Sec. E, p. 8.

"This is a remarkable book. Its mood is sustained throughout the narrative, which is briefly interspersed with inner monologues of the old man and the youth as the story progresses."

B648 Hall, Dorothy. Park East News (N.Y.C.), February 7, 1974, p. 5.

The repeated idea that words must be used as weapons against evil, individuals, situations and death is stressed. The reviewer says that the author does the job splendidly "with compassion, poetry and sensitivity."

B649 Hirschl, Bee. "'Merlin' Masters Control," Pittsburgh Press, January 13, 1974, Sec. H, p. 6.
Wiesel is called a Merlin of modern literature. "A sorcerer who can evoke formless terrors spawned in the mysticism of centuries past from the flesh and blood disasters of our lifetime." The mood of rising tragedy in the book is focused on in the review citing Wiesel as a master in control at all times.

B650 Hogan, William. "Elie Wiesel ... The Survivor." San Francisco Chronicle, December 18, 1973, p. 41.
The Oath is called "a haunting fable." The review is partly a lecture notice of an upcoming talk by the author in San Francisco.

B651 Horwitz, Carey. Library Journal, XLVIII (July 1973), 2157.
Positive review. Says "Wiesel characteristically relates suffering and destruction to optimism and life."

B652 Kaplan, Howard M. "Wiesel's The Oath Retells Old Story of 'Scapegoat' Jews." Denver Post, December 30, 1973, Roundup Sec., p. 40.
Compared to B. in J., The Oath is much more understandable for the reader who is not a student of mysticism or Hasidism.

B653 Kelso, Dorothy H. "Wail for the Dead." Boston Herald Advertiser, December 30, 1973, Sec. 3, p. 52.
The protagonist Azriel is spoken of as the archtypical Wandering Jew. As the book progresses, this reviewer says the sectarian aspects are abandoned. "He writes of common cause, of man's plight in the universe--in toils of Evil, unaided by God ... on fiction's sterile and burnt-out soil, Elie Wiesel strikes his rod and summons forth new life."

B654 Kirsch, Robert. "Oath to a Destroyed Town." Los Angeles Times, January 2, 1974, Sec. 4, pp. 4, 12.
Faults the novel in a literary sense, calling it "overwritten, pretentious, stylistically self-indulgent and didactic to the point of sactimony." The reviewer says that Wiesel is not the final arbiter of his own material. "He leaves the reader unclear as to how

man knows whether his visions are the will of God or the babblings of a madman."

B655 Leviant, Curt. "Wrestling With Demons." Saturday Review/World, I (January 12, 1974), 49-50.
The meanings of the name Kolvillag--Everyvillage--and the Jews--Everyman--are used as the focus of the discussion of the village as a microcosm of planet earth, and with its destruction, all of civilization is destroyed. "The Oath displays Wiesel's mastery of the Jewish tradition. He knows every nuance of Yiddishkayt." Marion Wiesel's translation receives fine praise.

B656 Margolies, Rabbi Morris B. "The Voice of Humanity Violated." Kansas City (Mo.) Star, December 9, 1973, Sec. E, p. 3.
The Oath is termed Wiesel's finest achievement. The scene of the burning of Kolvillag is cited as a vision of horror, a glimpse of the future. "It is a future Elie Wiesel hopes may be averted. He has harnessed his incomparable pen to that hope. He cannot stop. He is under oath to continue. For that we may be humbly grateful."

B657 Morley, Patricia. "Choosing Life." Ottawa Journal, February 2, 1974, p. 32.
"The mystery of silence remains a mystery, for all Wiesel's reflections. The novel's strength lies in its tale of the life and death of a town and its people. It shows that cruelty defeats itself, that murder is suicide. Wiesel opts for life."

B658 *Newton, Virgil Miller, Jr. "Book Views and Reviews." Tampa (Fla.) Tribune and Times, January 20, 1974.
"Superb reading if you can face up to the fact that we humans have been guilty of pogroms."

B659 Perlman, Milton B. "Booknotes." East Midwood Jewish Center (Brooklyn, N.Y.) Bulletin, January 18, 1974, p. 6.
The book is said to be written with overwhelming realism in a disturbing minor key. He says that the novel is fully demonstrative of the need for active, sympathetic response in the world today.

B660 Ridley, Clifford A. "Elie Wiesel: The Artist as Witness." National Observer, January 5, 1974, p. 15.

The review concentrates on the questions raised by the book, and the indifference of the world to them. A review of Wiesel's cantatta Ani Maamin is also included.

B661 Rosenberg, Ann. "Power and Agony of a Soul on Fire." Philadelphia Inquirer, December 23, 1973, Sec. H, p. 10.

Comparison to Camus appears in this positive review. Wiesel's first-hand authority in dealing with his topics is referred to here as well.

B662 Ryan, Frank L. Best Sellers, XXXIII (February 1, 1974), 478.

An astute summary. The reviewer feels there is negative feelings in the narrative voice, which he attributes to Mr. Wiesel's view of the world as that of the scholar and not that of the novelist. He feels the narrative voice and point of view shift so often in the novel that: "Events become reduced to mere manifestations of great forces and the humans become masks, soon transparent, behind which one sees the author's wrath, enthusiasm, sorrow."

B663 *Rye, Jack A. Sacramento Bee, December 23, 1973.

A short descriptive review.

B664 Siegel, Jack. Wisconsin Jewish Chronicle, December 21, 1973, pp. 34-35.

A largely negative review. The novel is compared unfavorably with I. B. Singer's A Crown of Feathers. He says, "Perhaps the time has come for Wiesel to take a giant step forward and deal in current reality. If he writes in the novel genre he should subject it to the norms of the form; not to rachmunis." Reprinted: *"Some Idle Thoughts and Rhetoric." Newark (N.J.) Jewish News, December 27, 1973.

B665 "Simple Plot--Complex Novel." Colorado West, February 17, 1974, p. 15.

The reviewer discusses Wiesel's complexity, his mastery of the art of drama, as well as his mastery of the art of creating atmosphere. Reading The Oath "with its intricate human detail of life in a Jewish village, its stories within stories, its wit and grace, is another haunting shattering experience."

B666 Srouji, Jacque. "Wiesel Holds Special Place." Nashville Tennessean, December 30, 1973, Sec. F, p. 14.
The theme of silence is stressed. What emerges from the novel is eternal hope and truth. A very positive review.

B667 Standen, Donna. "Torah Tells Survivor He Must Choose Life." Philadelphia Bulletin, January 27, 1974, Sec. 2, p. 3.
The concentration here is on the existential questions posed by the book. Wiesel is called "an intense writer who aims for our heart, our mind, our gut. His arrows rarely miss."

B668 Stern, Daniel. "From Autobiography to Myth, Experience to Metaphor." Hadassah Magazine, LV (December 1973), 20-21.
The themes of the author's previous books are traced. "The artistic journey from Night to The Oath is the journey from autobiography to myth; from experience to metaphor ... and its author has, once again, broken silence to bear witness."
Reprinted: "The World Testifies for the Dead." Nation, CCXVIII (January 5, 1974), 24-26.

B669 Task, Arnold S. "Feeling What Wiesel Feels." Greensboro (N.C.) News, February 17, 1974, Sec. B, p. 3.
Comment is made on the profound observations found in all of Wiesel's books. The Oath has much to say about the meaning of life and death.

B670 Thomas, Phil. "Wiesel Novel Chronicles Genocide in Village." *Sheboygan (Wis.) Press, December 31, 1973.
The reviewer is the Associated Press book editor and his review appeared in many newspapers, cited below. It is a clear positive review--speaking of "muted terror" and Wiesel's strong prose.
Reprinted: "New Book News." *Waycross (Ga.) Journal-Herald, January 2, 1974; "Wiesel Writes from Terror to Pogrom." *Peekskill (N.Y.) Star, January 5, 1974; Rocky Mountain News, January 6, 1974, Star-

time Sec., p. 19; Amarillo (Tex.) News-Globe, January 6, 1974, Sec. D, p. 2; *Wincester (N.Y.) Sun, January 12, 1974; *Gary (Ind.) Post Tribune, January 13, 1974; Detroit News, January 20, 1974, Sec. F, p. 5; *Mesa (Ariz.) Tribune, January 25, 1974; "Ultimate Horror of a Pogrom." *Bridgeport (Conn.) Post, February 3, 1974; Shreveport (La.) Times, February 3, 1974, Sec. F, p. 15; *West Memphis (Ark.) Times, February 6, 1974; "Hate Destroys Jewish Village." Savannah (Ga.) News, February 17, 1974, Sec. F, p. 5; *"Wiesel Writes Terror." Paris (Tenn.) Post Intelligencer, February 27, 1974.

B671 Washburn, Martin. The Village Voice, December 27, 1973, p. 17.
"The enormity of the theme of holocaust has destroyed the reality of many small towns in literature. Kolvillag must also be welcomed as their survivor."

B672 Weinberg, Helen. "The Liturgical Elie Wiesel." Cleveland Plain Dealer, December 16, 1973, Sec. H, p. 7.
The book is termed "liturgical." It is likened to the others in its "incentatory mystical echoing prose." In a discussion of the silence theme, the reviewer states that "life and language must win over death and silence."

B673 Weisman, John. "Who Can Bear or Bury ... the Truth?" Detroit Free Press, January 13, 1974, Sec. C, p. 5.
The collective responsibility that is required of a community for its actions is dealt with here; relation with Watergate is noted. Wiesel's stylistics make The Oath a multilevel novel like B. in J. It is called both chronicle and dream. "The chronicle of a dream, a dream of death." Ultimately, the book is an oeuvre of life, not death.

B674 Wieseltier, Leon. "History as Myth." Commentary, LVII (January 1974), 66-67.
Credits The Oath as an attempt by Wiesel "to bring his project to self-consciousness." By turning history into legend, this reviewer feels the horrors of the Holocaust are subordinated to an aesthetics of mystification which rob them of their force. He feels that Night was powerful because it was fresh. "The

Oath is rife with mythology.... It is in fact, its very content, whereas memory is frightfully dim."

B675 Wood, Michael. "Victims of Survival." The New York Review, XXI (February 7, 1974), 10-12.

The Oath is reviewed along with A Crown of Feathers and Other Stories, by I. B. Singer, and Somewhere, Perhaps by Amos Oz.

The reviewer traces the survivor theme as treated by the three authors. He feels that Wiesel's subject is powerful, but the book does not measure up. "Wiesel is a delicate and intelligent writer, but the tidy formality of his language keeps on letting him down, causes drastic falsifications of the questions he wants to ask. Everything is in memory, everything is in silence, the world divides into two symmetrical abstractions, a riddle for bookish school boys."

ANI MAAMIN

B676 Barra, Allen. "Wiesel Retells Old Tale." Birmingham (Ala.) News, February 17, 1974, Sec. E, p. 7.

"Ani Maamin moves Wiesel one step closer to the Nobel Prize."

B677 *Cincinnati Enquirer, February 17, 1974.

A short descriptive review.

B678 *El Paso (Tex.) Times, February 17, 1974.

Summary review.

B679 "Elie Wiesel's Ani Maamin: Cantata Powerfully Effective." Detroit Jewish News, February 22, 1974, p. 5.

The work is termed effective in both narration and text.

B680 Margolies, Rabbi Morris. "The Poetry of Faith." Kansas City (Mo.) Times, February 8, 1974, p. 34.

The poetic retelling of a Talmudic tale--Wiesel's first venture into verse form is spoken of. Wiesel's driven quality is made much of. "Usually the end of the road for men thus afflicted is insanity or, at the least, despair. Not so with Wiesel. He is the prototype Jew; the homo religious, the Jew who cannot stop his Ani Maamin chant, not even at the gates of gehenna.... He doesn't blaspheme in the ordinary sense--he is in the class of those who defy God because they believe in Him, children in spirit of the man called Job."

B681 Meacham, Harry M. "Wiesel Retells Talmudic Tale in Contemporary Setting." Richmond (Va.) New Leader, February 27, 1974, p. 13.
It is called a highly dramatic story even without the music.

B682 Shannon, Francis P. "Facing World, God." New Haven Register, February 10, 1974, Sec. D, p. 4.
Positive review. Mention is made of the Haggadah and of waiting for the Messiah.

REVIEWS OF BOOKS by Wiesel--French, Hebrew, Other Editions.

LA NUIT

B683 Bulletin (International Writers Association for the U.N.), Nos. 1 and 2 (June/July 1959), 17.
French review of La Nuit.

B684 Feigelson, Ralph. "La Nuit." Paris La Presse Nouvelle, October 31-November 1, 1959, p. 1.

B685 Neher, Andre. Elie Wiesel "La Nuit." Evidences, No. 76 (March 1959), 48.

L'AUBE

B686 "L'Aube." Figaro Littéraire, No. 739 (June 18, 1960), 15.

B687 Bulletin Critique du Livre Français, XVI (March 1961), 191.

B688 Chavardes, Maurice. France Observateur, July 7, 1960, p. 20.

B689 Petit, Henri. "Elie Wiesel L'Aube: Deux Hommes Devant la Mort." Parisien Libéré, June 7, 1960,

p. 6.

B690 Philippon, Henri. "Un Histoire Emouvante." Paris Jour, June 8, 1960, "Les Livres," p. 14.

B691 *Rudel, Yves-Marie. Ouest-France, July 12, 1960.

B692 *Vandercammen, Edmond. Bruxelles La Cité, June 9, 1960.

B693 Varennes, Jean-Charles. "L'Avenglante Vérité de l'Homme." Centre-Matin, January 6, 1960, "Les Lettres." p. 8.

B694 *Ziegler, Jean. Gazette Lausanne, July 9, 1960.

LE JOUR

B695 Bulletin Critique du Livre Français (Paris), XVI (May 1961), 363.

B696 Daoust, René ptre. "Le Jour." Relations, No. 253 (January 1962), 26.

B697 "La Fin d'un Traumatisme." La Terre Retrouvée (Paris), May 15, 1961, p. 6.
Le Jour is reviewed along with Aux Bords Verdoyants de la Spree by Hanz Scholz.

B698 Fontaine, André. "Le Jour." Le Monde, May 27, 1961, p. 9.

B699 "Les Livres." Bulletin du Cercle Juif (Montreal), (June-July 1961), p. 2.

B700 Nachor, Asher. "Siach Im Nishamot Matot." Tel Aviv Yidiot Achronot, May 26, 1961, 7 Yamin Sec., p. 6.
Hebrew review of Hebrew translation of Le Jour.

B701 *Wintzen, René. "Du Crepuscule des Dieux à la Lumière du Jour." Témoignage Chrétien, June 2, 1961.

LA VILLE DE LA CHANCE

B702 Aubery, Pierre. French Review (Baltimore), XXXVII (May 1964), 703-704.
A French review of La Ville de la Chance.

B703 Bulletin Critique du Livre Français, XVIII (March 1963), 212.

IR HA MAZAL

(Tel Aviv: Am Oved, 1963; Hebrew translation of the French: La Ville de la Chance)

B704 *Ag'f, M. "Ir Ha Mazel." Hayrut, December 7, 1964.

B705 Barzel, Hillel. "B'Mazel Shel Siutahai Gahennom." Tel Aviv Yidiot Achronot, December 13, 1963, p. 14.

B706 Ben-Menachem, Naftali. "Ka-alov B'Ofanah V'Ir Ha Mazel." Tel Aviv Hatzofeh, December 20, 1963, p. 5.

B707 Cohen, Ruth. "Ir Ha Mazel." L'Marchav, January 17, 1964, pp. 1, 2.

B708 Meged, Matti. "Du Siah Im Ha'Mavet." Tel Aviv Amut, February/March 1964, 95-100.
Essay-review on Ir Ha Mazel with a recapitulation of the previous books.

B709 Nahor, Asher. "Vi Kuach I'm Ha Ribonoh Shel Olom." Tel Aviv Yidiot Achronot, February 11, 1962, p. 16.

B710 "Olomo Ha Misucsach Shel Polit Ha Shoah." Tel Aviv Omer, December 20, 1963, p. 6.

B711 *Rut, D. "Michael Hanirdaf." Tel Aviv Mariv, December 24, 1963.

IM SAHAR
(Ha Lailah, Ha Sachar, Ha Yom; Tel Aviv:
Ktzin Chanuch Roshi, 1964; Hebrew translation by
Chaim Guri and Yeshyahu Ben-Porat of the French trilogy)

B712 Ardon, Ora. "L'chiot v'Lo L'Chiot." Masah, June 26, 1964, pp. 1-2.

B713 Avishi, Mordechi. "Misapar Tzair Kotev Al H'Shoah." Omer, March 5, 1965, p. 6.

B714 Cannan, Haviv. "Trilogia Al Ha'Mavet." Ha Aretz, September 4, 1964, p. 10.

B715 Namon, Yorom. "Elohim Ohev M'torfim." Davar (Tel Aviv), December 6, 1963, p. 9.
A review of Im Sachar and Ir Ha Mazel.

LES PORTES DE LA FORET

B716 Beck, Theodore Toulon. "French Fiction." Books Abroad, XXXIX (Autumn 1965), 425.
"The author mingles the real and the spiritual world skillfully and poetically."

B717 Bulletin Critique du Livre Français, XIX (November 1964), 1105.

B718 Daiches, David. "After Such Knowledge." Commentary, XL (December 1965), 105-110.
He calls Wiesel's novels great documents which must haunt everyone old enough to have lived through World War II.

B719 Grall, Xavier. "Lyrisme, Prophétisme, Simplicité Cantique à Melilla." Le Monde, No. 6154 (October 28, 1964), 10-11.

B720 *"Les Portes de la Forêt." Nouveau Candide, September 3, 1964.

B721 Saporta, Marc. "Le Mur est Partout." L'Express, No. 698 (2-8 November 1964), 58.

B722 Sungolowksy, Joseph. "Les Portes de la Forêt." French Review (Baltimore), XL (December 1966),

432-433.

SHAARE HA YAAR
(Hebrew translation from the French
of Les Portes de la Forêt)

B723 Avishi, Mordechi. "Eiyar Savlut Ha Yihudim." Mozniyim, May 28, 1967, p. 245.
An essay-review with background material on Wiesel that also features a review of the novel.

B724 ______, "Roman Ha'Shoah V'hagoral Ha'Yihudi." Omer, October 13, 1967, p. 4.
A comprehensive review of Shaare Ha Yaar. The same page also features a review of Yehudi Ha Dmama.

B725 Baron, Menachem. "Ha'Melim Ha'Aniot." L'Marchav, April 7, 1967, p. 5.

B726 Selker, Don. "Pa-anoach Yotzeh Dofen Shel Ha Shoah." Ha Aretz, April 17, 1967, p. 10.

B727 Shochm, Haim. "Ha'Givod Ha Boded Mul Ha Shoah." Yidiot Achronot, April 21, 1967, p. 18.

B728 Zahavi, A. "Gilgulov Shel Nitzul Ha'Shoah." Ha Yom, April 21, 1967, p. 5.

LES CHANTS DES MORTS

B729 *Alain, Jean-Claude. "Le Poids des Morts." Réformes (Paris), September 17, 1966.

B730 *Arnothy, Christine. "Les Lettres le Chant." Oise Matin, July 12, 1966.
*Reprinted: Le Parision Libéré, 12 Juillet 1966.

B731 *Aymon, Jean-Paul. "Elie Wiesel, Rescapé des Camps ou le Plaidoyer des Morts." Le Droit de Vivre (Paris), July 1966.

B732 Bentata, Leon. La Voix Sifharade (Lyon), No. 35 (November 1966), 9-10.

B733 Bulletin Critique du Livre Français, XII (October

1967), 815-816.

B734 Burncoa, Charles. "Récits." Les Nouvelles Littéraires, No. 2029 (July 21, 1966), 4.

B735 *Centre Presse Berry Republicain, August 17, 1966.

B736 Chase, Kathleen. Books Abroad, XLII (Winter 1968), 76.
"The book is valuable because it reminds us never to forget."

B737 *Elle, July 1967.

B738 Fabre, A. L'Education Nationale (Paris), No. 809 (December 15, 1966), 30.

B739 Gentily, A. M. "Le Tutoiement." La Terre Retrouvée (Paris), No. 648 (October 1, 1966), 7.

B740 Haedens, Kleber. "Les Pas et Les Cris Etouffés des Amis Perdus." Paris Presse l'Intrausigeant, June 18, 1966, Sec. D, p. 5.
A lengthy in-depth review.

B741 Kattan, Naim. "Elie Wiesel: Legendes et Prières." Le Devoir (Montreal), August 6, 1966, Sec. 2, p. 10.

B742 Le Clic'h, Guy. "Elie Wiesel Entre la Mort des Siens et la Vie des Autres." Le Figaro Littéraire, No. 1051 (June 9, 1966), 4.

B743 *Le Oiendional la France, August 29, 1966.

B744 Mandel, Arnold. "Le Chant des Morts." Information Juive, No. 167 (October 1966), 6.

B745 *"Response a 'Treblinka'" Le Chants des Morts. Le Republicain Lorrain, July 12, 1966.

B746 Saporta, Marc. "Entre Auschwitz et Hiroshima." La Quinzaine Littéraire, No. 9 (July 15, 1966), 7.

B747 "Vient Dé Paraitre." Le Monde, June 4, 1966, 10.

B748 *Ziegler, Jean. Coopération (Suisse), December 10,

1966.

YEHUDI HADMAMA
(Hebrew translation of Les Juifs de Silence)

B749 Avishi, Mordechi. "Yehudi Hadmama." L'Marchav, January 12, 1968, p. 6.

B750 Bornstein, Z. "L'Zoak et Yehudi Hadmama." Maariv, November 28, 1967, p. 20.

B751 ______. "Yehudi Hadmama." L'Marchav, November 29, 1967, p. 3.

B752 Friedlander, Yosef. "Yehudi Hadmama." Ha Yom, October 25, 1967, p. 5.

B753 Niv, M. "Yihudi Hadmama Zoakim." Maariv, October 27, 1967, p. 18.

B754 Numburg, Menachim. "Ha Yahadut Shanigzar Aliah Elaim." Tel Aviv Saarim, February 2, 1968, p. 5.

B755 Rivlin, Abraham. "Yehudi Hadmama." Ha Poel Hatzair, No. 3 (October 17, 1967), 20.

B756 Saltzman, Dorit. "B'Machatzitom Shel Yihudi Hadmama." Al Ha'Mishmar, September 3, 1967, p. 3.

B757 Vest, B. "Yehudi Hadmama." Davar, November 13, 1967, p. 3.

B758 "Zaakat Hadmama." Yidiot Achronot, September 29, 1967, p. 20.

ZALMEN OU LA FOLIE DE DIEU
(Reviews of the Play as published)

B759 Bulletin Critique du Livre Français, XXIII (July 1968), 606.

B760 *"Elie Wiesel Aborde le Théâtre." La Tribune de Lausanne, April 7, 1968.

B761 Mandel, Arnold. "Zalman ou La Folie de Dieu."

Information Juive (Paris), No. 182 (April 1968), 8.

B762 Saporta, Marc. "Vertu de la Folie: Zalmen ou la Folie de Dieu." La Quinzaine Littéraire (Paris), No. 50 (May 1-15, 1968), 12-13.
In addition to an in-depth review of the play, this account contains material on previous books.

B763 "Vient de Paraître." La Terre Retrouvée (Paris), No. 4 (December 1, 1968), 5.

B764 *Ziegler, Marie-Claire. "Elie Wiesel: Un Témoin de l'Horreur." La Gazette Littéraire (Paris), July 6, 1968.

LE MENDIANT DE JERUSALEM

B765 Amos, E. "Ha Misholet M'Yerushalyim." Hatzofeh, August 8, 1969, p. 4.
A Hebrew review of the Hebrew translation of Le Mendiant De Jerusalem.

B766 Avishi, Mordechi. "Ha Misholet M'at Eli Visel." L'Marchav, November 7, 1969, p. 7.
A Hebrew review of the Hebrew translation of Le Mendiant De Jerusalem.

B767 Baux, Dominique. "Elie Wiesel: Le Mendiant de Jérusalem." Etudes, CCCXXX (January 1969), 130-132.

B768 Beaupere, R. Lumière, XVIII (July-October 1969), 123.

B769 Duranteau, Josane. "Les Contes de la Sagesse." Les Lettres Françaises, No. 1260 (December 4-10, 1968), 11.

B770 Hahn, Pierre. "Prix Medicis: Elie Wiesel." Magazine Littéraire, No. 24 (December 1968), 19-20.

B771 Kolbert, Jack. "Elie Wiesel: Le Mendiant de Jérusalem." French Review (Baltimore), XLIV (October 1970), 189-190.
The reviewer states that the Holocaust theme has transcended the confines of Jewish literature and must

LA NUIT, L'AUBE, LE JOUR
(Paris: Editions de Seuil, 1969)

B781 Le Bulletin du Livre (Paris), No. 171 (November 1969), 36.

B782 *Monnoyer, Maurice. "La Mort à sa Porte." Nord-Eclair (Paris), January 9, 1970.

B783 Quinzaine Littéraire, No. 83 (November 16-30, 1969), 30.

B784 "Une Trilogie: La Nuit, L'Aube, Le Jour." Dialogue (Montreal), 1 (March-June 1962), 4.

B785 Weinberg, Henry H. "Elie Wiesel: La Nuit, L'Aube, Le Jour." French Review (Baltimore), XLIV (April 1971), 975-976.

This reviewer scores Le Jour as the most accomplished of the three, technically. In a general statement on the fiction of Wiesel he speaks of the link that keeps a man who has escaped death chained to it forever. He probes the question of what distinguishes Wiesel from the many other authors who have written on the holocaust. His conclusion: "Wiesel's concentration camp experience is above all a medium for the exploration of the universal theme of the tragedy of human existence."

CELEBRATION HASSIDIQUE

B786 *Allouche, Jean-Luc. "Célébration Hassidique." Le Rayol, April 1972.

B787 Ben-Ya-aKov M. "Sifarim Hadashim." Ha-Aretz (Tel Aviv), February 11, 1972, p. 14 (Overseas edition).

A Hebrew review of the French edition.

B788 Editions du Seuil (Paris), No. 155 (January 1972), 4.

A publication booklet by the publishing house reviewing the book.

B789 Ertel, Rachel. "Dans la Tradition Yiddish." La Quinzaine Littéraire (Paris), No. 116 (March 16-31, 1972), 6-8.

be regarded as one of the universal topics of contemporary French fiction. Wiesel writes, he continues, in the French language "with consummate f nesse."

B772 *Malka, Victor. "Elie Wiesel et le Destin Juif." Reforme, October 26, 1968.

B773 Memmi, Albert. "Le Mendiant de Jérusalem, par Elie Wiesel." Le Nouvel Observateur, No. 211 (November 25-December 1, 1968), 41.

B774 Misrahi, Robert. "Prix Medicis. Le Mendiant de Jérusalem." La Quinzaine Littéraire, No. 62 (December 1, 1968), 4-6.
In addition to a comprehensive review of the novel, this account also contains a lengthy essay review on the earlier works.

B775 Moeykens, D. "Le Mendiant de Jérusalem, Prix Medicis." La Revue Nouvelle, XLIX (January 1969), 104-105.

B776 Rawicz, Piotr. "Medicis: Elie Wiesel un Enfant de Genocide." Le Monde, No. 7424 (November 26, 1968), 28.

B777 Ricaumont, Jacques de. "Le Prix Medicis à Elie Wiesel. Changer le Malheur." Les Nouvelles Littéraires, No. 2149 (November 21, 1968), 3.

ENTRE DEUX SOLEILS

B778 "Elie Wiesel: "Entre Deux Soleils." La Libre Belgique, No. 191 (July 10, 1970), 7.

B779 Lapouge, Gilles. "Elie Wiesel, Le Témoin." La Quinzaine Littéraire, No. 99 (July 16-31, 1970), 14-16.

B780 Poliakov, Leon. "Les Interrogations d'Elie Wiesel." Le Monde, No. 7964 (August 22, 1970), 11.

This comprehensive review also contains a French bibliography on Hasidism.

B790 Harmon, Rachel. "Fraven Hasidut Ma Oshiut Un Gashtoltn fun Eli Visel." Unzar Vort (Paris), January 22, 1972, p. 5.
A Yiddish review of Célébration Hassidique in a Yiddish-French newspaper.

B791 Lazar, David. "Chasidut: Al M'Pat Ha Olom." Maariv (Tel Aviv), March 14, 1972, p. 33.
See review by Y'aaqov Haramgaal in American Zionist on Souls on Fire. (B564)

B792 Mandel, Arnold. "Le Hassidisme à la Splendeur Multiple." L'Arche (Paris), No. 179 (January 26-February 25), 70-71.

B793 Pytel, Roman. "Zopowiesci Chasydzkich." Folks-Sztyme (Warsaw, Poland), May 27, 1972, p. 1-2.
A Jewish-Polish newspaper in Polish. A lengthy review of the book. Note: An article on Saul Bellow appears elsewhere on the page.

B794 *Rondeau, M. J. "Elie Wiesel Célébration Hassidique." Bibliographie, December 1972.

LA SERMENT DE KOLVILLAG

B795 Rittel, Régina. "Le Silence et la Parole." L'Arche, No. 195 (May 26, 1973), 64-65.

DOCTORAL DISSERTATIONS

B796 Bernstein, Derora. "How Shall We Sing the Lord's Song in a Strange Land: The Journey Back to Life in the Midrash of Elie Wiesel." Dissertation Abstracts, XXXIV (November 1973), 2607A. (Ohio University)
Wiesel's vision of man is explored. Time, legend, spirit and dialogue are studied to show Wiesel's view of life in a post-Holocaust world. "On the journey back from the Holocaust hell, time transforms, legend liberates, spirit sustains and dialogue opens the fu-

ture. The characters and the books themselves journey back to the world of the living, bearing flowers from hell."

B797 Knopp, Josephine Zadovsky. "The Trail of Judaism and the Code of Mentshikhkayt in the Contemporary Jewish Novel." Dissertations Abstracts, XXXII (December 1971), 3312A. (University of Wisconsin)
Singer, Roth, Malmud as well as Wiesel use the theme of Judaism on trial. Wiesel is mentioned for his particular writing on the Holocaust and the aftermath.

MEDIA NOTICES--Radio (Zalman ou la folie de Dieu; a play)†

B798 [no entry]

B799 Combat (Paris), March 16, 1968, Weekend Section, p. 2.

B800 La Croix (Paris), March 14, 1968, p. 6.

B801 "France-Culture." Le Monde, March 8, 1968, Des Loisirs, p. 5.
Comprehensive preview of radio production.

B802 Mercoeur, Antoine. "Les Ondes Inspireés." Les Nouvelles Littéraires (Paris), No. 2120 (April 18, 1968), 2.

B803 Michel, Marcelle. "La Radio Diffusion." Le Monde, April 2, 1968, p. 16.

B804 *Seine-et-Marne Matin, March 9, 1968.

B805 *La Semarle, March 9, 1968, Radio Tele Sec.

B806 *Telerama, March 10, 1968.

B807 *La Vie Catholique Illustreé, March 6, 1968.

MEDIA NOTICES--Television

B808 *Eureka Times-Standard (Cal.), March 12, 1972.

---

†Production by "France-Culture" on French radio in March 1968.

An advance writeup for an upcoming T.V. book review show in the California area where Wiesel will be interviewed in connection with Souls on Fire.

B809 Kissel, Howard. Women's Wear Daily, April 4, 1972, p. 18.
A review of the T.V. program, "Sighet Sighet." This production of Elie Wiesel's recent visit to the central European town of his birth is highly praised. "It was remarkable, because it showed how powerful can be the impact of the spoken word." Mr. Kissel goes on to say: "Wiesel more than any other contemporary writer has given the word a new importance. His writing is a demonstration of belief in the power of words to recreate, to move, to redeem."

B810 ________. Women's Wear Daily, May 22, 1972, p. 14.
A review of the hour long show by Wiesel called "Itinerary," produced by the "Eternal Light."

MEDIA NOTICES--Motion Pictures

B811 Nathan, Paul. "Rights and Permissions." Publishers Weekly, CXCVII (January 12, 1970), 45.
An article on the difficulties of translating the melancholy and painful subject matter of Night to the screen.

B812 Ornstein, Bill. The Hollywood Reporter, CCXIV (February 5, 1971), 1.
A film of Wiesel's Beggar in Jerusalem is in production with Translor Productions. Much economic and production information is given.

B813 Weiler, A. H. "Choosing Beggar." New York Times, January 31, 1971, Sec. 2, p. 15.
A notice of the projected filming of Beggar in Jerusalem.

MEDIA NOTICES--Stage (The Madness of God)[†]

B814 Christopher, Anthony. Montgomery County (Md.) Sentinel, May 9, 1974, Sec. B, p. 2.

The Arean Stage actor, Richard Bauer, who plays the role of Zalman the madman in the play, says of Wiesel: "But in that Wiesel is a mystic, the play is a mystical tract, rather than a social tract, concerning a specific incident. Wiesel says that it is a dream of his." He calls the play a song. "And it's one of God's favorite songs, because its been sung so many times and in so many languages. Our job is to sing it not for our own kicks, but the best way we can, because if its sung very well, then God can't help but cry! And maybe He'll do something about it."

B815 Coe, Richard L. "'Madness of God' a Beautiful Play." Washington Post, May 10, 1974, Sec. D, p. 3.

The play receives plaudits from Mr. Coe on many levels. In speaking of the playwright he says: "The play becomes engrossing because Wiesel refuses to keep it on realistic ground. He finds allusions for what is within." The dramatic material contained in the rabbi's confrontation with the inspector is termed very fine. "The war of words is between this world and the invisible next. Fancy is freely admitted. Perhaps Zalman [the mad beadle] is right; the rabbi never did interrupt the service. Ideas are conveyed without being exactly expressed. With briefer exposition the intended soaring will last longer."

B816 Friedman, Albert. "Wiesel in D.C.: A Disturber of Our Peace." The Jewish Week and American Examiner, May 2, 1974, p. 2.

A profile piece in connection with the opening of "The Madness of God" at Arena Stage.

B817 Kernan, Michael. "A Witness to Solitude and Suffering." Washington Post, April 26, 1974, Style Sec., pp. 1, 7.

A profile of Wiesel in connection with a press con-

[†]World premiere, Arena Stage, Washington D.C., May 3, 1974 (through June 9, 1974).

ference highlighting the opening of the play "The Madness of God" at Washington's Arena Stage. Wiesel does not see himself a playwright, but a witness, nevertheless he is quoted as saying "We live in an age of theater in which the most important messages are being said, not in books, but on the stage."

B818 Richards, David. "How Faint a Cry is Never Heard." Washington (D. C.) Star-News, May 9, 1974, Sec. C, pp. 1, 7.
Says Wiesel's play "wants desperately to believe that man's words do indeed have a resonance that echoes long after the speaker has fallen silent. And yet, at the same time, it admits that the world is blanketed in a nightmare of quiet, muffling even the shrillest agony. It is this very ambiguity that makes 'The Madness of God' a tantalizing play, a difficult play, and ultimately a haunting play."

LECTURES, AWARD PRESENTATIONS and Other News Articles

B819 "Abraham, Jacob and Joseph to be Updated by Wiesel." Detroit Jewish News, October 27, 1972, p. 24.
An article on an upcoming visiting scholar weekend at Congregation Shaarey Zedek, November 2-5, 1972, at which Wiesel will be the recipient. "In his unique style Wiesel will create human portraits of figures of the past so that they appear as contemporaries."

B820 Aufbau (New York), January 5, 1973, p. 9.
A German newspaper of Jewish interest reports on Wiesel's appointment as visiting Distinguished Professor at the City College of New York.

B821 "Auschwitz Survivor, Author, to Speak Here." Cincinnati Enquirer, February 28, 1970, p. 6.
Biographical sketch for coming lecture at Adath Israel Congregation in Cincinnati.

B822 *"Author to Visit Valley." Van Nuys (Cal.) Valley News, February 11, 1972.
A preview of an upcoming talk by Wiesel at Temple Judea in Tauzana, California. Biographical informa-

tion and material on Souls on Fire is given. The author's "standing room only" lectures are noted.

B823 Bandler, Michael J. "Portrait of a Man Reading." Book World, December 26, 1971, p. 14.
The author Herman Wouk is being interviewed concerning his literary tastes. He comments: "and the best of the Jewish writers is Elie Wiesel. Nothing can compare with his Legends of Our Time and A Beggar in Jerusalem."

B824 Beam, Alvin. "Before You Hear Him on T.V., Here's Elie Wiesel." Cleveland Plain Dealer, February 27, 1972, Sec. F, p. 6.
A preview of an upcoming television show, "The Itinerary of Elie Wiesel as Seen from His Works." The article notes that Golda Meir will appear on the show in a "supporting role to the brilliant Jewish French-American novelist." Comments on Souls on Fire are given, along with noting future works--a novel The Fool, the Child and the Book [note: Now titled The Oath], and a book about Mrs. Meir.

B825 Bloom, Albert W. "Wiesel Sees the Holocaust In Its 'Agony and Artistry.'" Jewish Chronicle (Pittsburgh), November 7, 1968, p. 4.
A review of a lecture in Pittsburgh at the B'nai Israel Institute of Adult Jewish Studies. Wiesel is quoted as saying: "concern with the holocaust is the central historic and artistic experience of our Jewish future."

B826 Brother, Joyce. "Elie Wiesel: The Author and the Man." The Hillel Gate (Brooklyn College), III (November 1971), 1.
The reviewer calls the lecture by Wiesel an overwhelming experience for college students. Much mention is made of Wiesel's charisma, his views on Soviet Jewry, and on the holocaust. Wiesel on Judaism: "It contains beauty. It is up to the leaders to show this beauty to the uncommitted. We should do good things as a Jew--not under other titles."

B827 "... but for City University's Distinguished Professors; Enthusiasm Prevails." New York Times, December 23, 1972, p. 27.
An article on the Distinguished Professor program

at City College of New York. Wiesel's main problem has been his popularity, it is stated here. One hundred fifty students registered for his 8:30 a.m. class on "The Literary Responses to Persecution." In connection with his teaching Wiesel said: "I put in four hours of preparation for every hour I teach, because for each thing I say, I put my entire career on the line. That's a lot of time but you can't do it otherwise."

B828 City College Alumnus (New York), LXVIII (November 1972), 5.
Descriptive information about Elie Wiesel's course on the "Holocaust as Literature."

B829 Cohen, Edward. "Elie Wiesel." The Jewish Floridian, December 1, 1967, p. 8-A.
A review of Wiesel's talk in Miami. The reviewer discusses the existential nature of the address: "To be a Jew is to take upon one's self the whole Jewish past."

B830 "Community Gets Set to Greet Noted Author, Elie Wiesel." Jewish Observer of the East Bay (Oakland, Cal.), January 1972, p. 1.
Pre-lecture information, biographical material.

B831 Culmus. "People and Events: Vergelis v. Wiesel and Weill." World Jewry, XII (March/April 1969), 19.
A discussion of a disagreement concerning the publication of a shortened version of Jews of Silence.

B832 "Death Camp Survivor Tells Jews: Remember." Omaha World-Herald, February 17, 1972, p. 2.
In an address, Wiesel stressed the theme of the importance of studying the holocaust. He said, "Every killer kills twice--once when he kills and again when he tries to erase his act from your memory."

B833 "Ecrivain Juif, Ecrivain de Langue Française: Conférence de M. Elie Wiesel." Bulletin du Cercle Juif (Montreal), No. 73 (April 1962), 1.
La Dernière Réunion du Cercle Juif.

B834 Edelman, Lily. "Of Books." National Jewish Monthly, LXXXV (December 1970), 47.

A representative cross-section of Jewish writers, teachers and community leaders were polled for a survey for this magazine on the following question: "What are the three most exciting, important and/or stimulating books of Jewish interest you have read during the past year?" Elie Wiesel's books were mentioned most frequently in the responses.

B835 "Eitud Medalion Ha Hadoti L'Elie Vesel." Yidiot Achronot (Tel Aviv), May 7, 1972, p. 2.
An account of Wiesel winning the Medal of Freedom from The American Jewish Committee.

B836 "Elie Vesel Kibel B'Tzarfat B'Pras Medici L'Safrut." Maariv (Tel Aviv), November 26, 1968, p. 2.
Announcement of Prix de Medici by Paris correspondant of Maariv.

B837 "Elie Vesel Ketav 'Roman Ba-Pah' al Hashoah." Yidiot Achronot (Tel Aviv), April 11, 1972, p. 2.
A review of a talk Elie Wiesel gave at Yeshivah University in New York.

B838 "Elie Vesel Vert Bashtimt Oif Hoychan Akadamisan Amet." Der Algemeiner Journal (New York), September 29, 1972, p. 12. (in Yiddish)
Wiesel, who writes for this newspaper, is noted on receiving the Distinguished Professor appointment at the City College of New York.

B839 "Elie Wiesel Wins First Jewish Heritage Award." Publishers Weekly, CLXXXIX (April 4, 1966), 37-38.
Descriptive report of Award presentation of Jewish Heritage of B'nai B'rith for excellence in literature to Mr. Wiesel.

B840 "Elie Wiesel, Novelist Speaks of Needed Silence." The Font (Fontbonne College, St. Louis, Mo.), XLII (December 15, 1966), 2.
The reviewer reflects on hearing a Jew (Wiesel) speak about Auschwitz, and the effect it has on the Catholic mind. She was most impressed with the quality of silence and spirituality that Wiesel imparted.

B841 "Elie Wiesel Noted Author and Philosopher to be Park

Lecturer." B'nai Israel Scroll (Washington, D.C.), XXV (January 1970), 2.
A preview of a coming lecture on February 6, 1970, at the Synagogue. Much background information on Wiesel's career is given.

B842 "Elie Wiesel Is One of Avon's Most Popular Authors." Publishers Weekly, CCI (April 3, 1972), 49.
There are more than 765,000 copies of Wiesel's books in print in Avon covers.

B843 Fager, Charles. "Resistance in Prison on Rise--Berrigan." National Catholic Reporter, IX (January 5, 1973), 1, 17.
A report from Danbury, Connecticut, on the Rev. Philip Berrigan's release from prison. At a celebration following his release, Berrigan told a huge crowd a story by Wiesel. He told of the Jewish Just Man, who, when passing through the wicked city of Gomorrah didn't stop to look around, but continued on. Berrigan draws the following moral: "Those of us in the resistance are resolved not to be changed and absorbed by the evil of our society."

B844 "Famed Author Elie Wiesel at Brandeis, California." Jewish Voice (Cal.), November 25, 1966, p. 9.
Preview of talk with much biographical information.

B845 "Famous Author to Visit Hollywood." The Jewish Floridian, February 4, 1972, p. 1.
Pre-lecture information.

B846 Foster, Alice. Miami Herald, February 13, 1972, p. 12.
Same information concerning lecture as in preceding entry.

B847 Gaster, Jeff. "Wiesel Asks Jews: 'Are You Worthy?'" The Daily Pennsylvanian, October 15, 1971, pp. 1, 8.
In connection with the B'nai B'rith National Triennial Convention at which Wiesel was a featured speaker; his theme: "Are We worthy of fighting for Soviet Jewry and standing up for Jerusalem?"

B848 Goldberg, Max. "The New Elie Wiesel." Intermountain Jewish News (Denver), LIX (May 1972), 24.

A review from New York of Wiesel receiving the highest award of the American Jewish Committee--The American Liberties Medallion. Much of Wiesel's address is published in the article in addition to personal memoirs, and anecdotes about Francois Mauriac, Wiesel's patron in French Letters.

B849 Grand Rapids Press (Detroit), September 17, 1972, Sec. H, p. 1.
Article on cultural series that Elie Wiesel will initiate at Jewish Culture Council of Grand Rapids, October 15, 1972.

B850 Handler, M. S. "Lillian Helman is Among Nine Named to City University Chairs." New York Times, September 26, 1972, p. 38.
Wiesel's appointment as distinguished professor in the New York City University System is cited along with Lillian Hellman, Renata Adler, Rudolf Bing, Anthony Burgess, George Segal, Ulysses Kay, Edgar F. Borgatta, Herbert Arkin, and Edward Pesse.

B851 Hendler, Hannah. "Arab Jewry Living Out a Death Sentence." Genesis II (Cambridge, Mass.), April 20, 1972, p. 8.
This commentator feels that just as Wiesel pointed to the plight of Soviet Jews with his Jews of Silence, there is now a need for world Jewry to concern itself about the plight of Jews in Arab countries.

B852 Herschaft, Jean R. "Wiesel Condemns Apathy of Americans on War." The Jewish Post and Opinion (New York), XXXIX (May 12, 1972), 1.
A review of comments made at the American Jewish Committee's 66th Convention where Wiesel was given the American Liberties Medallion. He charged the American people with indifference calling it "no longer a sin but a punishment." He called on each Jewish organization to adopt a little city of Jewish remnants in Europe.

B853 "Hirek." Maramarossziget (Tel Aviv), February 1972, p. 4.
A Hungarian/Hebrew newspaper noting a talk by Wiesel at Brooklyn College.

B854 "Homage Paid to Rabbi Heschel by 500 at a Traditional Service." New York Times, December 25, 1972, p. 20.

The news report of Rabbi Abraham Heschel's funeral service included the following: A recitation by Elie Wiesel of "God Follows Me Everywhere," one of a group of Yiddish poems written by Rabbi Heschel as a young man in Warsaw in 1933.

B855 Huber, Gary. "Why Should We Remember." Nefesh (Ann Arbor, Mich.), II (November 1971), 3.

Wiesel is featured in a college paper whose current issue is devoted to the holocaust. He is quoted as having found meaning in the destruction, and this reviewer excerpts the following from Wiesel's remarks on what is to be learned from Auschwitz: "This perhaps may be our mission to the world: We are to save it from self-destruction."

B856 Hunter, Anna. "Award." Savannah News, May 2, 1965, Magazine sec., p. 8.

A news article on the book page telling of the Jewish Book Council award to Elie Wiesel for T.B.T.W.

B857 Hurwitz, Donald. "The Silence Between Question and Answer." Together, I (March 1974), 7-8.

In the journal of the B'nai B'rith Hillel Foundation of the University of Maryland, a student editor gives his impressions of an encounter with Wiesel in conjunction with Wiesel's lecture on campus on February 7, 1974. Much material on silence, and on the impression Wiesel makes on youth.

B858 Hyer, Marjorie. "Young Jews Obsessed by WWII." Washington Post, October 22, 1972, Sec. F, p. 8.

A report by a writer for the L.A. Times-Washington Post Service of a talk Wiesel gave in Washington, D.C., at the Klutznick Exhibit Hall of the B'nai B'rith Building. The talk was in connection with the opening of a photographic exhibit prepared by Yad Vashem, Israel's National Remembrance Authority, to commemorate the 30 years that have passed since the Nazi terror. Wiesel's remarks commented on the current persecution against Soviet Jews and the ransoms they are forced to pay if they wish to leave for Israel. This ransom was compared to the attempts during WWII to try to reduce Jews to objects. "They can persecute us, they can even kill us, but they can't reduce us to objects." Reprinted: Tri-City Herald (Pasco, Washington), November 1, 1972, p. 12; *Advance (Staten Island), October 29, 1972.

B859 Jewish Floridian. "Wiesel Calls for Action as 1,500 Salute Academy," January 12, 1973, p. 4-B.
At a talk at the Hebrew Academy of Miami, Mr. Wiesel "roundly condemned the organized missionary efforts of fundamentalist Christian groups and the 'Jesus Freaks.'"

B860 Jewish Teachers' Association Newsletter, January 1973, p. 1.
An announcement of the joint forthcoming Avodah and Morim awards by the Jewish Teachers' Association to Elie Wiesel and Louis Kaplan, to be awarded on March 25, 1973. A large biographical section is included with the announcement.

B861 Jewish Telegraphic News Bulletin, XXXIX (October 17, 1972), 3.
A descriptive account of Wiesel's address at B'nai B'rith on October 16, 1972. (B857)

B862 "Jewish Writer Tells of Nazi Holocaust." Worcester (Mass.) Telegram, March 7, 1972, p. 11.
In a lecture, Wiesel stressed his existential theme: "Anything that happens in the world is related to the holocaust."

B863 Kass, Marcia. "Stirring Up the Past." Argue/Dimension, February 15, 1974, p. 3.
Ms. Kass, a student editor of the University of Maryland magazine, reviews her impressions of Wiesel and covers his lecture at the University of Maryland. "Wiesel must love people a lot to get up in front of apathetic and cynical students and make a polemic for awareness and concern."

B864 Lewis, Theodore N. "From the Rabbi." Temple Topics (Brooklyn, N.Y., Progressive Shaari Zedek Synagogue), XXV (November 8, 1971), 2.
An account of a lecture given by Wiesel at Brooklyn College on October 12, 1971 (Post Simchat Torah night). He spoke mainly of Soviet Jewry and read from Jews of Silence. The reviewer states: "This was indeed an extraordinary evening. The challenge

to American Jewry not to forget their Soviet brethren rings in my ears."

B865 Macchello, Ronda. "Four Responses to 'Evil' Outlined." Palo Alto (Cal.) Times, June 5, 1972, p. 16.
Professor Robert McAfee Brown in a mini-course at the 40th annual Campus Conference of the Alumni Association cited Wiesel along with Dietrich Bonhoeffer, Daniel Berrigan, as examples of the ways in which human beings confront evil.

B866 Mekaton, Dave. "Elie Wiesel: A Holocaustal Hesse." The Livingston Medium, December 3, 1970, p. 7.
A pre-lecture essay on Wiesel, comparing him to other existential writers. Material on books to date is also given.

B867 Moss, Elli. "Jewish Novelist Speaks on Mystic Judaism Branch." The Florida Alligator (Gainesville), December 3, 1972, p. 4.
At a talk at University of Florida, Mr. Wiesel spoke in connection with a tour for Souls on Fire. He is quoted as saying: "The Hasidic masters are really our contemporaries ... what preoccupies them preoccupies us, whatever haunts them haunts us."

B868 Mount Sponsors Lecture by Major Jewish Writer." Riverdale Press (Bronx, N.Y.), March 22, 1973, p. 1.
Preview article on a Wiesel lecture to be given at the College of Mount Saint Vincent on March 28, 1973, on the theme: "Confronting Evil: The Human Challenge of Our Times."

B869 "New Baritone on the Horizon." The Jewish Post and Opinion, XXXVIII (November 19, 1971), 5.
A news report on Wiesel, who, instead of delivering a talk at the oneg-shabbat at the General Assembly of the Council of Jewish Federations and Welfare Funds in Pittsburgh sang shabbat zemeros and told Hasidic tales.

B870 "Notes on People." New York Times, April 3, 1973, p. 39.
A news article on Wiesel's appointment as a regular member [he had previously been a visiting Dis-

tinguished Scholar] of the Faculty of the City College of New York with the rank of full professor.

B871 Peckham, Stanton. "Reader's Roundup." Denver Post, March 15, 1970, Roundup, p. 18.
A report of a speech that Wiesel made in Denver's Temple Emanuel to a crowd of over 1,000. The reviewer compares Wiesel to I. B. Singer, and he mentions the rapid sale of Beggar in Jerusalem and Wiesel's other books during the time of the author's appearance.

B872 Platt, Judy. "Wiesel Praises '2nd City,'" Canadian Jewish News (Toronto), June 2, 1972, p. 12.
In an address, Wiesel praises Toronto as his second favorite city, following Jerusalem. Much of the address is an evocation of images of Jerusalem.

B873 *Polsky, Barry. "Wiesel Sees Judaism Surviving in Russia." Jewish Week, December 8, 1966.
Speaking at the B'nai B'rith Board of Governors, Wiesel stated that Jewish history takes place whenever Jews are suffering and that Jewish history today "is therefore taking place in the Soviet Union rather than in Israel or America where Jews are free." He also spoke about his visits to Russia in 1965 and 1966.

B874 Postal, Bernard. Jewish Week, November 30, 1973, p. 15.
"Elie Wiesel, interpreter of the Holocaust will be among the nominees for the 1973 Nobel Prize for Literature."

B875 Rackman, Emanuel Rabbi. "Jews Without History?" Jewish Week, October 5, 1972, p. 15.
Rabbi Rackman takes an idea from Souls on Fire to develop his thesis in his feature article. He points to the parable that Wiesel uses which illustrates the possibility that we are no longer able to tell the story. Rabbi Rackman says this is the core of the problem of Jewish identity. He uses the book as an example of the quest for Jewish identity which he believes begins with the study of Jewish history.

B876 Raymont, Henry. "French Literary Awards Given to Two Writers Who Live in U.S." New York Times,

November 26, 1968, p. 44.
News report of the Prix Medicis for Beggar in Jerusalem.

B877 "The Real State of the World." Nation, CCXIV (June 12, 1972), 741.
An editorial article on Elie Wiesel's appearance as commencement speaker at Manhattanville College in Purchase, New York. The college, until recently, has been a Catholic institution for young women. The comment was made in the editorial that the citation given to Wiesel spoke much truth. It read: "To a world flooded with the tenuous reality of facts, you celebrate the truth and magic of man's imagination, of his awesome power to tell stories."

B878 Rogow, Sally. "Wiesel Offers Vision of Jewish Survival." Jewish Western Bulletin (Vancouver), February 27, 1970, p. 8.
In a lecture review this reporter concentrates on Wiesel's truth, which she sees as the truth of the holocaust, with Wiesel as its witness.

B879 Rosove, John. "Wiesel: A Personal View." The Jewish Radical (Los Angeles), April 1972, p. 10.
A warm positive essay commenting on Wiesel's appearance at the Brandeis Institute for a group of Los Angeles Jewish leaders. The reviewer spoke of how effectively Wiesel was able to communicate the feeling of the burden that he carries.

B880 Rothchild, Sylvia. "Elie Wiesel in Boston." Boston Jewish Advocate, CXLIII (November 16, 1967), Sec. 2, p. 15.
Wiesel spoke of the world that forgot. The reporter felt that the audience was moved not so much by the words but by the "sight of a super-sensitive human being."

B881 Rotstein, Menahem. "Where Are Your Professors?" Genesis II (Cambridge, Mass.), III (November 4, 1971), 2.
A review of a Wiesel lecture for the Combined Jewish Philanthropies of Greater Boston. He spoke of a lack of leadership for today's Jewish youth.

B882 Schumach, Murray. "Wiesel Urges Graduates to

Have Faith." New York Times, May 28, 1972, Sec. A, p. 14.

A report on Wiesel's commencement address at Manhattanville College May 27, 1972. He is quoted: "I have learned the meaning of certain words which then become offerings. I have learned that man must ultimately be a link. My idea in my story telling is to make Jews better Jews, and Christians better Christians, and in general, if possible at all, make man a little bit warmer, so he will not feel crushed by his own solitude."

B883 Schwartz, Rabbi Frederick C. Mount Zion Temple Bulletin (St. Paul, Minn.), January 16, 1970, pp. 1-2.

A review of a lecture at the Union Biennial by Wiesel, where he addressed himself to the following question: "How can we speak of the holocaust?"

B884 Schwartz, Leo W. Jewish Book Annual, Vol. XXIII. New York: Jewish Book Council of America, 1965-1966, 233-234.

Presentation of the Harry and Ethel Daroff Memorial Fiction Award of the Jewish Book Council of America to Elie Wiesel for his novel, Town Beyond the Wall.

B885 Scimone, Frank A. "Wiesel, Burgess Among 50 Named Distinguished Profs." Clarion (New York), II (November 30, 1972), 1, 6.

A union newspaper of the Professional Staff Congress of the City University of New York welcomes Professor Wiesel to its membership. In speaking about the union aims, Wiesel stated: "I am all for professors and teachers to join together in order to achieve the same purpose, to elevate the standards of teaching and to achieve a higher condition for their students." In commenting on his students, Wiesel said he found them "knowledgeable and very sophisticated."

B886 Seidman, Hillel Dr. "The Jew Who Becomes a Voice for Our Conscience." The Jewish Press (New York), September 1, 1972, pp. 10, 16.

A response to an attack by Rabbi Meir Kahane on Elie Wiesel in the Jewish Press of June 9, 1972, in which Kahane states that Wiesel doesn't do enough for

Soviet Jewry. Dr. Seidman adamantly points to all of Wiesel's work for Soviet Jewry and calls Kahane's attack baseless.

B887 Shatin, Judith. "Wiesel's Novel: The Silence Which is Past Words." Caellian (Douglass Collage Newspaper), December 4, 1970, p. 5.
Background material in preparation for a lecture at Rutgers University by Wiesel on December 7, 1970.

B888 Shenker, Israel. "Mrs. Meir Aware of 'Image' Crisis by Israel." New York Times, October 7, 1969, p. 15.
A report of a social gathering at the apartment of Elie Wiesel in Manhattan. Mrs. Meir was the honored guest, commenting on her visit with President Nixon. Wiesel, in presenting Mrs. Meir to his guests, told of her moving appeal to the late President John F. Kennedy for arms with which to defend Israel.

B889 Siegel, Jack. "Elie Wiesel ... Guilt ... The 6 million." The Jewish World (Schenectady, N.Y.), May 4, 1972, p. 1.
This reporter challenges a statement of Wiesel's made at a speech in New York City in which he [Wiesel] charged the American Jewish leadership with silence and failure in 1942-43 to come to the aid of the Jews in Nazi concentration camps and forced ghettos. Mr. Siegel feels that the guilt for the holocaust does not rest with Jewish leadership. "It is not the fault of survivors. It is universal." Concerning Wiesel he continues, "Wiesel may be a talented writer and considers it his ministry to be a consciousness-raiser, but his burning soul is not necessarily the torch to lead us, and our youth, through the guilt ridden, shadowed alleyways to the right road of redemption and Jewish realization." [Letter to the Editor concerning the above article appeared in the May 11, 1972, issue of The Jewish World by Mrs. Ethel Pincus Horwitt of Stockbridge, Mass.] She takes Jack Siegel's article to task by showing mistakes in his knowledge of American Jewish history during the war years. She says: "Elie Wiesel is right--American Jewish leadership knew all about the wholesale slaughter and was silent. Was the Z.O.A. afraid the American Jew couldn't take it?"

B890 Silverman, Jan. "Voice of the Six Million." Oakland Tribune, March 5, 1972, Entertainment Sec., p. 29.

An account of a lecture by Wiesel at the Kaiser Center under the auspices of the Jewish Welfare Federations of Almeda and Contra Costa Counties. The stories Wiesel told at the lecture are commented on, along with his thoughts on the troubles in the world. His literary style, way of life and new books that he is working on, are discussed as well. A personal comment by the author is included. He believes in reading three books at a time--a novel, one on philosophy and another for research. "Otherwise one becomes plunged into one universe, which is not healthy. It is better to balance several facets of life."

B891 Sky, Doris. "Huge Crowd Thrilled by Wiesel Address." Intermountain Jewish News (Denver), March 28, 1969, Sec. A, p. 14.

At this lecture in Denver, Wiesel makes mention of the holocaust as an underlying cause for student rebellion. He connects the theme of all of today's turmoil with Jewish history.

B892 Smulyan, Ruth. "Reunion in Syracuse." Syracuse Herald-Journal, December 3, 1972, p. 20.

A preview of an upcoming lecture.

B893 Speyer, Bess and Broadd, Greg. "Greatest Jewish Writer-Speaker Elie Wiesel Set for November 7; Capacity Crowd Expects 'Moving Experience of Conscience.'" Jewish Review (Tulsa), XLI (October 1971), 1.

A huge buildup for an appearance by Wiesel in Tulsa, Oklahoma.

B894 Spotts, Leon H. Jewish Education, XXXVIII (October 1968), 49.

Wiesel was guest speaker at the 42nd Annual Conference of the National Council for Jewish Education held on May 12-15, 1968, at Grossingers, N.Y. He spoke of Israel as but one of three centers of concern for American Jewish Education. The other two areas are the Nazi Holocaust, and the Jews of Sorrow (behind the Iron Curtain).

B895 Taft, Adon. "Jewish Protests Flare As Key 73 is

Launched." Miami Herald, January 13, 1973, Sec. AA, p. 2.

A report on Jewish protest to program of evangelism undertaken by some 140 Protestant and Catholic denominations. Quotes are given from Wiesel's address to the Miami Hebrew Academy where the reviewer states that Wiesel put especial blame on the Catholic Church for what he claimed was its role in the escape of Nazi War Criminals at the end of the fighting. (B858)

B896 Time, XLIX (June 12, 1972), Education Section, 41.

Remarks quoted from address given at the commencement exercises of Manhattanville College.

B897 Tolchin, Martin. "Hostility Toward Jews Decried at Emergency Conference Here." New York Times, May 16, 1972, p. 46.

At an emergency conference in New York City, called to draw attention to the mounting hostility toward Jewish civil servants and other professions, Wiesel expressed his extreme concern. "I don't like what's happening to me. From the tensions that I feel tonight, I'm frightened," he said. "I tell you, it disturbs me deeply."

B898 "Too Late for Sorrow, Wiesel Says at D.C. Exhibit on Holocaust." The Jewish Week, October 19, 1972, p. 1.

A report on Wiesel's appearance as featured speaker at B'nai B'rith Building for the opening of a photographic Holocaust Exhibit prepared by Yad Vashem (see B857). Picture included showing government and international dignitaries in audience. Reprinted: The Youngstown (Ohio) Jewish Times, October 27, 1972, p. 1; *Intermountain Jewish News (Denver), October 27, 1972; *Wisconsin Jewish Chronicle, October 26, 1972; Jewish Ledger, October 27, 1972, p. 13. *Texas Jewish Post, October 26, 1972.

B899 "Two French Literary Prizes are Awarded to Americans." New York Times, May 30, 1963, p. 15.

A news report of the Prix Rivarol Award for four novels written in French, awarded to Elie Wiesel.

B900 Village Voice (N.Y.C.), XVII (April 6, 1972), 45.

A news article announcing the Holocaust Memorial

Day commemoration to be held April 10, 1972, at Yeshiva University. Elie Wiesel will be the speaker and the event is in remembrance of the Warsaw Ghetto Revolt.

B901 Weberman, J. M. "Elie Wiesel at C.C.N.Y." Ha Magen, II (December 19, 1972), 1. [newspaper of the Jewish Studies Department of the City College of N.Y.]

A review of the first lecture by Wiesel as visiting professor on Hasidism. When asked about his new role as professor, Wiesel replied, "It's a new experience and I learn a lot from my students; they are really very good."

B902 Wee, David. "Fiction as Event." Event, February 1972, p. 32. [Syracuse University student newspaper].

This reporter speaks of the religious feeling he experienced in hearing Wiesel speak. In speaking of the novels he continues, "they put you in the grip of a deeply spiritual man who has suffered beyond belief and lived to give us his vision of a people."

B903 Weisman, John. "Storyteller Elie Wiesel Weaving His Spell at a Local Synagogue." Detroit Free Press, March 12, 1972, Sec. B, p. 5.

A review of a lecture at Congregation Shaaray Zedek in Southfield, Michigan. The adulation of the young is noted--their desire to touch him. The large audience consists of many young people from Ann Arbor, Lansing and Flint. "The young see in him something they don't often see in their parents: a man who has totally accepted his tradition, his past. He is--a Jew. That is his life. They can read his works and see, not just an accumulation of words, but a total philosophy." Reprinted: Los Angeles Times, April 16, 1972, Calendar Sec., pp. 1, 52, 60.

B904 "Wiesel: 'I Plead for the Dead.'" Metropolitan Star [B'nai B'rith Publication, N.Y.], June 1968, p. 8.

Review of B'nai B'rith Convention talk at the Concord Hotel, Kiamesha Lake, N.Y., May 27, 1968. Theme of the address was pleading for the dead. The talk was prior to publication of L.O.O.T.

B905 "Writings of Wiesel, Other Jewish Authors Available."

Tulsa Daily World, November 7, 1971, Sec. A, p. 3.
A display of works by Wiesel at the Tulsa Central Library is noted in preparation for Wiesel's upcoming appearance in Tulsa.

B906 "Young Russian Jews Winning, Author Says." _St. Louis Globe-Democrat_, December 7, 1971, Sec. A, p. 9.
At a lecture in St. Louis, Wiesel said, "Young Jews in Russia are winning their battle with song and dance rather than bloodshed."

B907 Ziprin, Nathan. _B'nai B'rith Messenger_, December 12, 1969, pp. 33, 37.
A review of a party Mr. Wiesel hosted for visiting Prime Minister Golda Meir. In reply to Mr. Wiesel's remarks concerning her previous visit to the late President Kennedy, Mrs. Meir stated, "If I had been able to speak to the President as beautifully as Elie Wiesel, I might have gotten much more."

AUTHOR/REVIEWER INDEX
(All citations will be understood to be to the "B" listings)